WORD Among Us

A Worship-centered, Lectionary-based
Curriculum for Congregations

Learner's Guide for Older Youth

Year 2

United Church Press

Cleveland, Ohio

Thomas E. Dipko	Executive Vice President, United Church Board for Homeland Ministries
Ansley Coe Throckmorton	General Secretary, Division of Education and Publication
Lynne M. Deming	Publisher
Sidney D. Fowler	Editor for Curriculum Resources
Kathleen C. Ackley	Associate Editor for Curriculum Resources
Monitta Lowe	Editorial Assistant
Marjorie Pon	Managing Editor
Kelley Baker	Editorial Assistant
Cynthia Welch	Production Manager
Martha A. Clark	Art Director
Lynn Keller	Business Manager
Paul Tuttle	Marketing Director
Angela M. Fasciana	Sales and Distribution Manager

Writers

Ted Huffman, writer of the lessons for Proper 17 through Advent 4, is co-pastor of Wright Congregational Church UCC in Boise, Idaho, where he enjoys sharing learning with youth and adults.

Janet Comperry Lowdermilk is adjunct professor of theater at Lees College, Jackson, Kentucky. Janet wrote the lessons for Christmas 1, Epiphany 1 through Epiphany 3, Pentecost Sunday through Proper 6, and Proper 8 through Proper 16.

Carol Birkland, an experienced Christian educator and writer of educational resources, lives in Cleveland, Ohio, and works as a professional journalist. Carol wrote the lessons for Christmas 2, Epiphany 4 through Transfiguration Sunday, and Easter 2 through Easter 7.

Kelly Boyte Peters, writer of the lessons for Lent 1 through Easter, is senior minister of Avon Lake United Church of Christ, Avon Lake, Ohio. She has written for *Discipleship Alive!*, *Disciple Magazine*, and *United Church News*.

Editors

Laurel Hayes, a former campus minister, is currently a doctoral candidate in religion and education at Union Theological Seminary and Teacher's College/Columbia University. She is approved for ordination in the United Church of Christ. In addition to editing, she wrote the lesson for Proper 7.

Kelly J. Ackley has edited educational materials for six years. She serves on the children's education committee at St. Paul and St. Andrew United Methodist Church in New York City.

Deborah Rose taught high school English and edited secondary school textbooks prior to her ordination in the United Church of Christ. She served churches in New England and is currently studying for a doctor of ministry degree.

United Church Press, Cleveland, Ohio 44115
© 1995 by United Church Press

Design

Kapp & Associates, Inc., Cleveland, Ohio

Cover art

Glen Strock, *Rapture at Rio Arriba*, detail, Dixon, New Mexico. Used by permission.

Suddenly, unexpectedly, God's future reign breaks in on the community of Rio Arriba. The surprised villagers are lifted out of their ordinary lives and into a new way of being.

Glen Strock, *Rapture at Rio Arriba*, Dixon, New Mexico. Used by permission.

Welcome and Information Sheet

During this year you and your friends can also expect to be surprised by God through the study of the Word as you learn and grow together with *Word Among Us*. You will come to know that you are a part of God's own people as you think and dream about your own life. As you respond to the Word, you may find yourself making new commitments and new promises. As you study the Bible readings of the lectionary, your experience of worship will be enriched, lifting you beyond the ordinary to unexpected heights. Enter this new experience curious, expecting, and open. God will meet you there!

To help your leaders nurture the group, please complete the form below and return it to them.

Name ....

Address ....

Phone ....

Birth date ....

Year in school ....

Parent(s) or guardian(s) ....

Address ....

Phone ....

Have you been baptized? If so, when and where? ....

....

If you were baptized as an infant, have you been confirmed? If so, when and

where? ....

What are your special interests or hobbies? ....

....

....

What talents or information would you be willing to bring to this group?

....

What are your hopes for this group? ....

....

....

....

Contents

Invite the **Forgotten**

Jesus said also to the person who had invited him, "When you give a luncheon or a dinner, do not invite your friends or your brother or sister or your relatives or rich neighbors, in case they may invite you in return, and you would be repaid. But when you give a banquet, invite those who are poor, crippled, lame, and blind."

Luke 14:12–13

Edward Hopper, *Nighthawks*, oil on canvas, 1942, Friends of American Art Collection, 1942.51, photograph © 1994, The Art Institute of Chicago. All rights reserved. Used by permission.

It is night in the city.

Where do the nighthawks gather?

Where is safety, food, a welcome place?

FORGOTTEN

Who are the forgotten?

Study this painting for a minute, then look away. What details stick in your mind? Are there any unexpected guests at the table? Does the scene in the painting remind you of similar scenes from your own experience?

Jack Baron *The Picnic*, 1989, Key West, Florida.
Used by permission.

Think of the "forgotten" in your school, your community, and the world. Write the name of each person or group you think of on a chair at the table. Say a prayer for each name you add.

Welcome!

We're gonna sit at the welcome table,

We're gonna sit at the welcome table

one of these days, hallelujah!

We're gonna sit at the welcome table.

We're gonna sit at the welcome table

one of these days.

All God's children around that table.

All God's children around that table

one of these days, hallelujah!

All God's children around that table.

All God's children around that table

one of these days.

Traditional Spiritual

Fearfully and Wonderfully Made

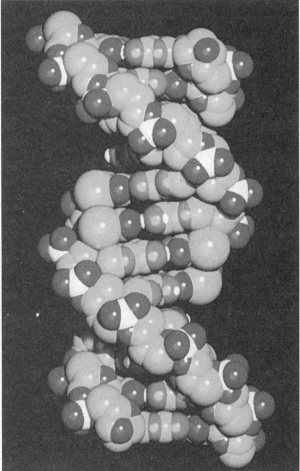

© 1995 Leonard Lessin/Peter Arnold, Inc., New York, N.Y. Used by permission.

Consider one of the smallest elements of our human makeup—DNA. What do you think about when you imagine such elements coming together to form you? What does it make you think about God?

I praise you, for I am fearfully and wonderfully made.

Psalm 139:14a

Psalm 139:1–6, 13–18

O God, you have searched me and known me!
You know when I sit down and when I rise up;
you discern my thoughts from afar.
You search out my path and my lying down,
and are acquainted with all my ways.
Even before a word is on my tongue,
O God, you know it altogether.
You beset me behind and before,
and lay your hand upon me.
Such knowledge is too wonderful for me;
it is high, I cannot attain it.
For you formed my inward parts,
you knit me together in my mother's womb.
I praise you, for you are fearful and wonderful.
Wonderful are your works!
You know me right well;
    my frame was not hidden from you,
when I was being made in secret, intricately
    wrought in the depths of the earth.
Your eyes beheld my unformed substance;
in your book were written every one of them,
the days that were formed for me,
    when as yet there was none of them.
How precious to me are your thoughts, O God!
How vast is the sum of them!
If I would count them, they are more than
    the sand.
When I awake, I am still with you.

Inclusive-Language Psalms (New York: The Pilgrim Press, 1987). Used by permission.

Soil for legs
Axe for hands
Flower for eyes
Bird for ears
Mushroom for nose
Smile for mouth
Songs for lungs
Sweat for skin
Wind for mind
Just enough.

Nanao Sakaki, in *Break the Mirror*
(New York: Farrar, Straus and Giroux,
1987). Used by permission.

Meinrad Craighead, *Changing Woman*, 1982, as reproduced in *The Mother's Songs* (Mahwah, N.J.: Paulist Press, 1986), 32. Collection of Myrna Little, Texas. © Meinrad Craighead. Used by permission.

The dream images of Meinrad Craighead often open the way to imagining the process of change— of fetus in womb; of psyche developing toward maturity; of the imagination itself making connections and growing.

Notice the layers that surround the woman in the image. What layers of change have you undergone since you were conceived and born? What changes are you experiencing now? Imagine the changes you will undergo in the future.

Seek, Find, REJÓICE

Woman Sweeping, from *Medieval Woman's Book of Days* (New York: Workman Publishing Co.). Used by permission.

When the woman has found the coin, she calls together her friends and neighbors, saying, "Rejoice with me, for I have found the coin that I had lost."

Luke 15:9

IF YOU WERE THIS WOMAN, WHAT

WOULD YOU BE LOOKING FOR?

WOULD YOU NEED A BROOM TO HELP

YOU FIND IT? OR WOULD YOU NEED

THE LIGHT THAT GOD PROVIDES?

Words and music: African-American spiritual

This lit-tle light of mine, I'm gon-na let it shine.

This lit-tle light of mine, I'm gon-na let it shine.

This lit-tle light of mine, I'm gon-na let it shine, let it

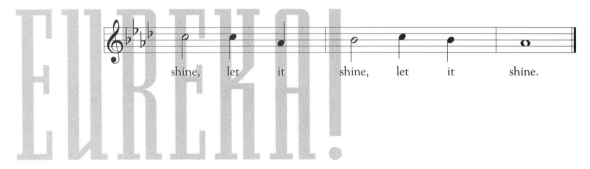

shine, let it shine, let it shine.

I TOOK THE PIECES YOU THREW AWAY AND PUT THEM TOGATHER BY NIGHT AND DAY WASHED BY RAIN DRIED BY SUN A MILLION PIECES ALL IN ONE

Bud Lee, *Reverend Howard Finster's "Paradise Garden" in Summerville, Georgia*, as reproduced in C. Kurt Dewhurst, Betty MacDowell, and Marsha MacDowell, *Religious Folk Art in America: Reflections of Faith* (New York: E. P. Dutton, 1983), p. 108, plate 133. Used by permission.

"EUREKA" means "I found it."

With scraps and thrown-away junk,

Finster creates his vision of Eden.

Where do you see something new

emerging from things that have

been lost or discarded?

GRIEVE WITH GOD

Hark, the cry of my poor people from far and wide in the land: "Is God not in Zion? Is Zion's Ruler not there?" (Why have they provoked me to anger with their images, with their foreign idols?)

Jeremiah 8:19

Like Jeremiah lamenting the destruction of Israel, God weeps for us. What are some of the specific reasons why God weeps for us today? How do you envision God weeping for us? How do you imagine God expressing grief for the world's pain?

Rembrandt Harmensz van Rijn, *Jeremiah Lamenting the Destruction of Jerusalem*, The Rijksmuseum, Amsterdam, The Netherlands.

SI FUI MOTIVO DE DOLOR, OH DIOS
IF I HAVE BEEN THE SOURCE OF PAIN, O GOD

Si fui motivo de dolor, oh Dios;
si por me causa el débil tropezó;
si en tus caminos yo no quise andar,
¡perdón, oh Dios!

Si vana y fútil mi palabra fue;
Si al que sufría en su dolor dejé;
no me condenes, tú, por mi maldad,
¡perdón, oh Dios!

Si por la vida quise andar en paz,
tranquilo, libre y sin luchar por ti
cuando anhelabas verme en la lid,
¡perdón, oh Dios!

Escucha oh Dios, mi humilde confesión
u líbrame de tantación sutil;
preserva siempre mi alma en tu redil.
Amén, Amén.

If I have been the source of pain, O God;
If to the weak I have refused my strength;
If, in rebellion, I have strayed away;
Forgive me, God.

If I have spoken words of cruelty;
If I have left some suffering unrelieved;
Condemn not my insensitivity;
Forgive me, God.

If I've insisted on a peaceful life,
Far from the struggles that the gospel brings,
When you prefer to guide me into strife,
Forgive me, God.

Receive, O God, this ardent word of prayer,
And free me from temptation's subtle snare,
With tender patience, lead me to you care.
Amen, Amen.

Sara M. deHall, based on a text by C. M. Battersby, trans. Janet W. May, in *The New Century Hymnal*.
English translation © Copyright 1992 by the Pilgrim Press. Used by permission.

Pablo Picasso, *Guernica*, Centro de Arte Reina Sofía, National Museum, Madrid, Spain (Giraudon/Art Resource, N.Y.). Used by permission.

Holy God,
holy and strange,
holy and intimate,
have mercy on us.

O my people, what have I done to you?
How have I offended you?
Answer me.

I brooded over the abyss,
with my words I called forth creation:
but you have brooded on destruction,
and manufactured the means of chaos.

O my people, what have I done to you?
How have I offended you?
Answer me.

I breathed life into your bodies,
and carried you tenderly in my arms:
but you have armed yourselves for war,
breathing out threats of violence.

O my people, what have I done to you?
How have I offended you?
Answer me.

. . .

Holy God,
holy and strange,
holy and intimate,
have mercy on us.

Janet Morley, "Holy God," in *Bread of Tomorrow*,
ed. Janet Morley (London: Christian Aid, 1992), 89–91.
Used by permission.

Shortly after Hitler's forces bombed this small Basque village during the Spanish Civil War, Pablo Picasso was commissioned by the Spanish Loyalist Government to paint this mural for the Paris World's Fair of 1937. Various interpretations have been offered for this work. Pain, dismay, despair, and anguish mark the six human faces, as well as that of the horse.

"Guernika," in *The Civil War in Spain, 1936–1939*, ed.
Robert Payne (New York: G. P. Putnam's Sons, 1962), 195–97,
quoted in Alberto de Onaindía, "Guernica Aflame,"
Picasso's Guernica, ed. Ellen Oppler (New York: W. W. Norton
and Company, 1988) 163–64.

God have mercy.
Christ have mercy.
God have mercy.

the WAY *of* FAITH

Pursue righteousness, godliness, faith, love, endurance, gentleness. Fight the good fight of the faith; take hold of the eternal life, to which you were called.

1 Timothy 6:11b–12a

Brian Bailey,
Rock-climbing,
Tony Stone Images,
Chicago, Illinois.
Used by permission.

Have you ever gone rock-climbing or mountain-climbing?

Imagine being in the position of the person in the picture.

Imagine the concentration, the steadiness, and the calm needed to climb safely.

Are there times when you feel like you're climbing a mountain,

looking for a place to take hold so that you won't fall?

Brian Bailey, *Rock-climbing*, detail, Tony Stone Images, Chicago, Illinois. Used by permission.

[A gift] my mother has given me is the understanding *La vida es la lucha*—The struggle is life. For over half my life I thought my task was to struggle and then one day I would enjoy the fruits of my labor. This is the kind of resignation and expectation of being rewarded in the next life that the . . . Church has taught for centuries. Then I began to reflect on what my mother often tells the family: "All we need to ask of God is to have health and strength to struggle. As long as we have what we need to struggle in life, we need ask for nothing else." This understanding gives me much strength in my everyday life. It has allowed me to be realistic—to understand that, for the vast majority of women, life is an ongoing struggle. But above all it has made me realize that I can and should relish the struggle. The struggle is my life; my dedication to the struggle is one of the main driving forces in my life.

Ada María Isasi-Díaz, "A Hispanic Garden in a Foreign Land," in *Inheriting Our Mothers' Gardens: Feminist Theology in Third World Perspective*, ed. Katie Geneva Cannon, Ada Maria Isasi-Diaz, Kwok Pui-Lan, Letty M. Russell (Philadelphia: Westminster, 1988), 99. Used by permission.

Have mercy
Upon us.
Have mercy
Upon our efforts,
That we
Before Thee,
In love and in faith,
Righteousness and humility,
May follow Thee,
With self-denial, steadfastness,
    and courage,
And meet Thee
In the silence.

Give us
A pure heart
That we may see Thee,
A humble heart
That we may hear Thee,
A heart of love
That we may serve Thee,
A heart of faith
That we may live Thee,

Thou
Whom I do not know
But Whose I am.

Thou
Whom I do not comprehend
But Who hast dedicated me
To my fate
Thou—

Dag Hammarskjöld, *Markings*, trans. Leif Sjoberg and W. H. Auden (New York: Alfred A. Knopf, 1966), 214–15. Translation © 1964 by Alfred A. Knopf, Inc., and Faber & Faber Ltd. Used by permission.

What does it mean to pursue...

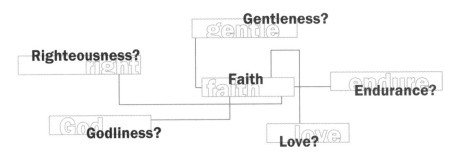

Righteousness?

Gentleness?

Faith

Endurance?

Godliness?

Love?

What are our responsibilities along each of these paths?

A Grandmother's Faith

I am reminded of your sincere faith, a faith that lived first in your grandmother Lois and your mother Eunice and now, I am sure, lives in you.

2 Timothy 1:5

Rick Reinhard, *Laying on of Hands*, Washington, D.C. © Rick Reinhard. Used by permission.

The Faith of the Bible's Young Timothy

Faith is what is handed down from mother to daughter to son . . . "a faith which was alive" in mother and daughter and which now lives in the child of the third generation.

Carl Holladay, "II Timothy 1:1–14," in Fred B. Craddock et al., *Preaching Through the Christian Year: A* (Philadelphia: Trinity Press International, 1992), 191.

Who has given their faith to you?

We celebrate the passing on of faith and courage from generation to generation.

The Legacy

They went together—those
wrinkled hands and tattered
book. And something in the
awe with which she held it
made me think she held
a sacred fire.

The old brass-bound Bible
came to her from her mother,
and hers before that, too,
through more generations than
I know how to reckon—faded,
cracked, worn with use.

I wonder how it felt to hold
the past within her hands—
how many broken hearts found
comfort there, how many searching
minds were fed; how many fears
were calmed in its reading; what
songs of joy were hummed over it;
what secret tears still stain its pages?

I loved to hear her talk to God,
and when she prayed, I sometimes
imagined I felt God near. It was a
very safe place to be—with God and
her.I liked her God, so wrapped up in
thesmall goings-on of daily life—not
toofar away and busy with eternal
things to take notice of one
small child.

The Bible became mine today, and
my smooth hands look somehow out
of place—and somehow right at home.
Like her, I hold the accumulated joys
and sorrows of my heritage and join
my life with theirs. There is a
strength to it—forged by faithful
living in the presence of a loving
God. The line still holds—all those
who have gone before, myself, and those
who are to come.

Marie Livingston Roy, *Accent on Youth*, vol. 17, no. 1
(Fall 1984): 3. Used by permission.

Archibald John Motley, Jr., *Mending Socks*, 1924, oil on canvas,
58.1.2801, Burton Emmett Collection, Ackland Art Museum,
University of North Carolina at Chapel Hill. Used by permission.

Love is a legacy, passed from

generation to generation.

What forms will the love and

faith you possess take when

passed to a new generation?

God's Awesome Deeds

Wakantanka Taku Nitawa
(Many and Great, O God, Are Your Works)

Text: Dakota hymn, Joseph R. Renville, 1842
Paraphrased by R. Philip Frazier, 1929; alt.

Tune: LACQUIPARLE
Native American melody (Dakota)
Adapted by Joseph R. Renville, 1842
Harmonization by J. R. Murray, 1877

All the earth worships you; they sing praises to you, sing praises to your name. Come and see what God has done; God does awesome deeds among mortals.

Psalm 66:4–5

Wa- kan- tan- ka, ta- ku ni- ta- wa tan- ka- ya
Man- y and great, O God, are your works, Mak- er of

qa o- ta; Ma- hpi- ya kin e- ya- hna- ke ca,
earth and sky; Your hands have set the heav- ens with stars,

ma- ka kin he du- o- wan- ca, Mni- o- wan-
Your fin- gers spread the moun- tains and plains. Lo, at your

ca śbe- ya wan- ke cin, he na o- ya- ki- hi.
word the wa- ters were formed; Deep seas o- bey your voice.

Optional hand-drum rhythm: ♩ ♩ ♩ ♩

Linda Lomahaftewa, *New Mexico Sunset*, detail, The Heard Museum, Phoenix, Arizona. Used by permission.

Does a sunset inspire you to "make a joyful noise to God"? Among God's awesome deeds, which do you celebrate? Why?

Canticle of the Sun

Linda Lomahaftewa, *New Mexico Sunset*, The Heard Museum, Phoenix, Arizona. Used by permission.

What images come to mind when you look at this painting? Psalm 66 is the psalmist's response to God's awesome deeds. St. Francis of Assisi wrote the "Canticle of the Sun" in praise of God's splendid creation. What words would you use for your own psalm of praise?

Be praised, my God,
for all your creatures,
and first for brother sun,
who makes the day bright and luminous.
And he is beautiful and radiant
      with great splendor,
he is the image of you, Most High.

Be praised, my God,
for sister moon and the stars,
in the sky you have made them brilliant and
      precious and beautiful.

Be praised, my God, for brother wind
and for the air both cloudy and serene
      and every kind of weather,
through which you give nourishment to your
      creatures.

Be praised, my God, for sister water,
who is very useful and humble
      and precious and chaste.

Be praised, my God, for brother fire,
through whom you illuminate the night.
And he is beautiful and joyous and robust
      and strong.

Be praised, my God, for our sister, mother earth,
      who . . . watches over us
and brings forth various fruits
      with colored flowers and herbs.

Be praised, my God,
      for our sister, bodily death,
from whom no living thing can escape.
Blessed are those whom she finds doing your most
      holy will. . . .
Praise and bless my God
and give thanks to God and serve God
      with great humility.
One instant is eternity;
eternity is the now.
When you see through this one instant,
you see through the one who sees.

St. Francis of Assisi (1182–1226)

Be praised, my God.

20

WORDS,

Sweeter than Honey

How sweet are your words to my taste, sweeter than honey to my mouth! Through your precepts I get understanding; therefore I hate every false way.

Psalm 119:103–104

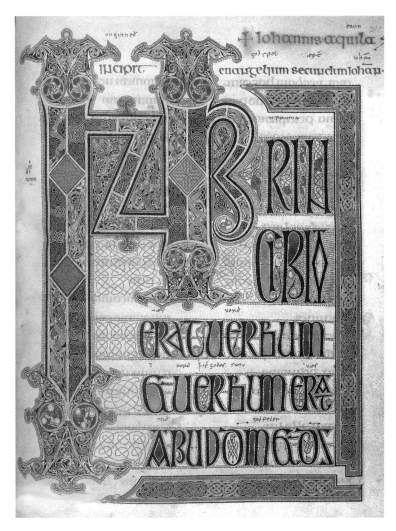

The Beginning of the Gospel of St. John, manuscript illumination from the *Book of Lindisfarne*, Cotton Nevo, D. iv, f. 211, The British Library, London, England. Used by permission.

In the ninth and tenth centuries Christian monks and priests spent long hours illustrating letters and words as they copied them onto sheets of vellum (refined sheep hides) to be made into books. There were no printing presses to record the Word of God. There were only a few skilled copyists who spent their whole lives making the words beautiful for the reader.

All words are spiritual—nothing is more spiritual than words.— Whence are they? along how many thousands and tens of thousands of years have they come? those eluding, fluid, beautiful, fleshless, realities, Mother, Father, Water, Earth, Me, This, Soul, Tongue, House, Fire. What beauty there is in words! What a lurking curious charm in the sound of some words!

Walt Whitman, *An American Primer*, ed. Horace Traubel (1904), abridged and reprinted in *Parabola* 8, no. 3 (August 3, 1993), 6.

What words of God do you carry in your heart?

Marc Chagall, *Moses Receives the Tablets from the Lord*, 1950–52, collection of the artist, St. Paul de Vence, France (Giraudon/Art Resource, N.Y.). Used by permission.

In this painting, God's hands reach down to Moses, who is reaching up to receive God's Words. How does God reach out to you? How do you reach out to God to receive God's Words? Name the ways God's Word makes a difference in your life.

God's Spirit Poured Out

Then afterward I will pour out my spirit on all flesh; your sons and daughters shall prophesy, your old men shall dream dreams, and your young men shall see visions. Even on the male and female slaves, in those days, I will pour out my spirit.

Joel 2:28–29

Spirit

S P I R I T

The Holy Spirit has been

compared to wind, fire, and

a dove. What image do **you**

have of the Holy Spirit?

Spirit, spirit of gentleness,
Blow through the wilderness, calling and free.
Spirit, spirit of restlessness,
Stir me from placidness,
Wind, wind on the sea.
You call from tomorrow,
You break ancient schemes,
From the bondage of sorrow
The captives dream dreams;
Our women see visions,
Our men clear their eyes,
With bold new decisions
Your people arise.

James K. Manley. All rights reserved. © 1978.
Used by permission.

23

A Litany of God's Spirit

Group 1: Your Spirit, O God, comes like tongues of flame.

Group 2: Your Spirit comes like water poured out on all.

Group 1: Your Spirit, O God, comes to rich and poor.

Group 2: Your Spirit comes to female and male.

All: Your Spirit is poured out on all.

Group 1: We celebrate your Spirit with our voices.

Group 2: We celebrate your Spirit with our minds and memories.

Group 1: We celebrate your Spirit with the work of our hands.

Group 2: We celebrate your Spirit with the love of our hearts.

All: We celebrate your Spirit, poured out for all.

Group 1: Come, Holy Spirit!

Group 2: Open us to the awareness of your presence.

Group 1: Sons and daughters will prophesy.

Group 2: Old ones will dream dreams.

Group 1: Young ones will see visions.

Group 2: Inspire us to envision a future of hope and peace and justice.

All: Splash upon your people. Wash us with faith and thanks.

Overflow from our lives.

Come, Holy Spirit. Amen.

Spirit.
poured out.

Zacchaeus, COME DOWN!

Jonathan Green, *Tales*, Jonathan Green Studios, Inc., Naples, Florida.
Used by permission.

Up *Where You Can See*

Sometimes you just gotta get up where you can see.
A short man climbed a tree.

Sometimes you just gotta get up where you can see.
Jesus called him down and entered his life.

Sometimes you just gotta get up where you can see.
It usually isn't that simple. Most people don't see things clearly the first time.

Sometimes you just gotta get up where you can see.
There are barriers which prevent real changes.

Sometimes you just gotta get up where you can see.
Dear God, open our eyes.

Sometimes you just gotta get up where you can see.
Dear God, open our minds.

Sometimes you just gotta get up where you can see.
Dear God, open our hearts.

Sometimes you just gotta get up where you can see.
Help us to get up where we can see you more clearly.

Sometimes you just gotta get up where you can see.

When Jesus came to the place, he looked and said to Zacchaeus, "Zacchaeus, hurry and come down; for I must stay at your house today." So Zacchaeus hurried down and was happy to welcome Jesus. All who saw it began to grumble and said, "He has gone to be the guest of one who is a sinner." Zacchaeus stood there and said to Jesus, "Look, half of my possessions I will give to the poor; and if I have defrauded anyone of anything, I will pay back four times as much."

Luke 19:5–8

We wear the mask that grins and lies,
It hides our cheeks and shades our eyes—
This debt we pay to human guile;
With torn and bleeding hearts we smile,
And mouth with myriad subtleties.

Why should the world be overwise,
In counting all our tears and sighs?
Nay, let them only see us, while
	We wear the mask.

We smile, but, O great Christ, our cries
To thee from tortured souls arise.
We sing, but oh the clay is vile
Beneath our feet, and long the mile;
But let the world dream otherwise,
	We wear the mask!

Paul Laurence Dunbar, in *The Complete Poems of
Paul Laurence Dunbar* (New York: Dodd, Mead, 1913).

Emil Nolde, *Hermit in a Tree*, 1931, Stiftung Seebull Ada und Emil Nolde,
Neukirchen, Germany. Used by permission.

the Mask

Up a Tree

What "drives you up a tree"?

What masks help to keep you there?

Jesus makes the same invitation to us as he

did to Zacchaeus, "Hurry and come down!"

Eternal Comfort, Good Hope

Now may our Lord Jesus Christ himself and God our Parent, who loved us and through grace gave us eternal comfort and good hope, comfort your hearts and strengthen them in every good work and word.

2 Thessalonians 2:16–17

Walter Williams, *Caged Bird*, The Amistad Research Center, New Orleans, Louisiana. Used by permission.

Why do you think this picture appears here alongside the passage from Second Thessalonians? If you are aware of Amnesty International, reflect on how the work of that organization may be suggested by this picture.

Be Like the Bird

**Be like the bird, who
Halting in his flight
On limb too slight
Feels it give way beneath him,
Yet sings
Knowing he hath wings.**

Victor Hugo, in *Illustrated Treasury of Children's Literature* (New York: Grossett and Dunlop, 1955), 133.

Prayer for Hope and Comfort

We gather, O God, aware that our world has many problems.
At times we are overwhelmed by the problems we see and
   hear about. We are confronted with stories of physical and
   sexual abuse, suicide, homicide,
war and starvation,
illness and accidents,
divorce, pregnancy,
failure and fear.
Sometimes we feel powerless to deal with our own problems,
let alone those of our friends, our community, and our world.
We ask you to lead us out of our feelings of helplessness.
Help us, loving God, to respond to life's challenges.
We need the encouragement of your eternal hope.
For ourselves and those we hope to help, we ask for comfort
   and for the strength that comes through faith in you.
We offer our lives to you, knowing that you hear and
   respond to our prayer. Amen.

Take heart.

An Encouraging Word

Make your own checklist of people who would welcome some
words of encouragement and perhaps a "good work." Think of
those as close as your own family as well as people far away.

_____ _____

_____ _____

_____ _____

_____ _____

In the next week or two, make a special effort to give
encouragement and hope to two or three of the people you
have listed.

Yet now take courage. . . . All you people of the land, says God; work, for I

am with you, says the God of hosts, according to the promise that I made

you when you came out of Egypt. My spirit abides among you; fear not.

Haggai 2:4–5

ENDURANCE

BY YOUR

Noel Counihan, *Homage to Goya: Requiem for El Salvador*, 1985, collection of Pat Counihan, Melbourne, Australia. Used by permission.

They asked Jesus, "Teacher, when will this be?" And Jesus said, "Beware that you are not led astray; for many will come in my name and say 'I am the one!' and, 'The time is near!' Do not go after them. You will be hated by all because of my name. But not a hair of your head will perish. By your endurance you will gain your lives."

Luke 21:7a, 8, 17–19

A CELEBRATION READING

Leader: Let us offer our lives to God.
Group 1: We live in tough times.
Group 2: We face real troubles.
SILENCE
Leader: Let us remember God's promise.
Group 1: God promises words that give life.
Group 2: God promises wisdom.
SILENCE
Leader: Let us give thanks for our lives.
Group 1: We have not perished.
Group 2: By endurance, we gain life.
SILENCE
Leader: Let us celebrate God's promise for hard times.
Group 1: The Spirit will not abandon us.
Group 2: Christ's abiding presence will support us.
SILENCE
Leader: Amen.
All: Amen.

This painting represents the artist's tribute to those in Latin America engaged in the struggle against oppression and his protest against all injustice. Both the figure and the title of the work refer to Goya's painting *The Third of May,* which depicted an instance of massive injustice in Spanish history.

Rosemary Crumlin, *Images of Religion in Australian Art* (Kensington, New South Wales: Bay Books, 1988), 100.

GOOD Words for TOUGH Times

Rembrandt Harmensz van Rijn, *Two Women Teaching a Child to Walk*, c. 1640, © The British Museum, London. Used by permission.

Learning to walk isn't easy! This child will fall many times before it confidently walks unaided. We stumble as we learn to walk in faith. Yet we can count on God to sustain us as these women are supporting this child.

"And remember, I am with you always, to the end of the age." —Matthew 28:20

"And now faith, hope, and love abide, these three; and the greatest of these is love." —1 Corinthians 13:13

"Blessed are you when people revile you and persecute you and utter all kinds of evil against you falsely on my account." —Matthew 5:11

"Heaven and earth will pass away, but my words will not pass away." —Luke 21:33

"The light shines in the shadows and the shadows did not overcome it." —John 1:5

"Just as I have loved you, you also should love one another." —John 13:34

"God is love, and those who abide in love abide in God and God abides in them." —1 John 4:16

"Then your light shall break forth like the dawn, and your healing shall spring up quickly." —Isaiah 58:8

In your patience
you will gain your souls.

Luke 21:19, Danish Bible of 1830

God
Remembers

Edward "Rainbow" Larson (designer) and Verla Shilling (quilter), *Missouri Farm, Newton County*, Santa Fe, New Mexico. Used by permission.

Then the child's father Zechariah was filled with the Holy Spirit and spoke this prophecy: "Blessed be the God of Israel, for God has looked favorably on God's people and redeemed them. God has shown the mercy promised to our ancestors, and has remembered God's holy covenant."

Luke 1:67–68, 72

Quilting is memory's art.

New fabrics combine with old skills to create a vision of the past in all its color, complexity, and texture. This quilt also reveals hopes for the future. What hopes do you see for the future in images from your past?

Prayer of Confession

Almighty God,

I come to you

because I am struggling inside.

I dwell on past hurts and heartaches

and refuse to let them go and forgive.

For that, forgive me.

I spend so much time as a worrier,

looking within,

that I forget the promise of your [child],

given for me.

For that I need forgiveness.

I focus too many times on useless

    speculation of the unknown

and fail to recall your promise

of the Holy Spirit.

Forgive me!

For not remembering that you . . .

live within and beside me

Forever.

Amen.

From the Sunday service of worship, International
Fellowship of Metropolitan Community Church,
Key West, Florida. Used by permission.

Symbol Prayer

Eternal God,
who in the time of Noah
gave us the rainbow
as a sign of promise,
bless this symbol
that it also may be
a sign of promises
fulfilled in lives
of faithful loving;
through Jesus Christ
our Savior.
Amen.

Book of Worship (New York: United Church
of Christ Office for Church Life and
Leadership, 1986), 335. Used by permission.

God is always faithful.

You are God's promise.

Live in Expectation

Keep awake therefore, for you do not know on what day your Lord is coming. But understand this: if the owner of the house had known in what part of the night the thief was coming, the owner would have stayed awake and would not have let the house be broken into. Therefore you also must be ready, for God's future Ruler and Judge is coming at an unexpected hour.

Matthew 24:42–44

Cross of the Community,
artisans of La Palma,
El Salvador.

This cross and others like it have been produced in El Salvador since the latter years of the civil war there. They are a part of a cottage industry that enables the people of El Salvador to have some economic power. The crosses are remarkable for their use of color and images of hope in a situation of despair. Scenes of their ordinary lives are painted on Christ's cross. The woman's figure at the center of the cross with her arms spread wide at once suggests the form of the crucified Jesus and the risen Christ who is embodied in the daily work and struggle of the Salvadoran people. In your day-to-day life, where do you want God to come?

Waiting in Wonder

God of wonder and surprises,
we, who are full of expectation,
wait in hope of the promises
of this season of gladness.

Christ, whose birth was foretold
by prophets full of wisdom
and words of challenge and comfort,
we trust in the promise of your coming.

Holy Spirit, by your power
Mary, who was full of grace,
became Mother of the Christ child,
waiting on God in prayerful expectation.

Eternal One, we look up from our everyday worries
as we wait in hope of your holy birth—
full of wonder and surprise—
in us.

Toda la Tierra
(All Earth Is Waiting)

All earth is waiting to see the Promised One,
And open furrows, the sowing of our God.
All the world, bound and struggling, seeks true liberty;
it cries out for justice and searches for the truth.

Mountains and valleys will have to be made plain;
open new highways, new highways for our God,
Who is now coming closer, so come all and see,
and open the doorways as wide as wide can be.

In lowly stable the Promised One appeared,
yet feel that presence throughout the earth today,
For Christ lives in all Christians and is with us now;
again, on arriving Christ brings us liberty.

Glen Strock, *Rapture at Rio Arriba*,
Dixon, New Mexico. Used by permission.

Rapture at Rio Arriba **whimsically depicts the suddenness of the end of time. The "unexpected hour" of God's future reign has broken in on the community of Rio Arriba, lifting them from their ordinary lives.**

A Dream of Peace

The wolf shall live with the lamb, the leopard shall lie down with the kid, the calf and the lion and the fatling together, and a little child shall lead them.

Isaiah 11:6

This painting depicts Isaiah's vision of peace. Look at the animals' expressions. Where are they looking? What might they be thinking? Put yourself in the picture. Where would you be in this peaceable kingdom?

We see glimpses of your peaceful creation.

Prayer for Peace

Gracious God, we see glimpses of your peaceful creation, and we can almost imagine what it would be like to live in a world where peace is the way of daily life.

Keep our imaginations alive and inspire us each day with visions of how we can help create peace. Don't let us just get used to the way things are.

Jesus taught that we should turn hostility into harmony by loving our enemies, by praying for those who give us a hard time. It's not easy to do that, God.

We need your help. Keep showing us ways to be peacemakers. Grant us your peace.

Amen.

A shoot shall come out from
    the stump of Jesse,
and a branch shall grow out of
    his roots.
The spirit of God shall rest
    on him,
the spirit of wisdom and
    understanding,
the spirit of counsel and might,
the spirit of knowledge and fear of God.

Isaiah 11:1–2

Here are two interpretations of Isaiah 11:1–2. How do they affect your understanding of these verses? What might your interpretation look like?

C. Terry Saul, *Tree of Jesse*, The Heard Museum, Phoenix, Arizona. Used by permission.

Root of Jesse

Root of Jesse
rising
from many an ancient prophecy

promised child
to all who would be reconciled
breaks through at last.

A virgin shoot accepts
God's seed
bows to the Mighty Deed.
One branch
bears bud, flower, fruit:
Christ blossoms as David's root.

Lord, you are stem, stalk, tree!
Let your fruit take root in me.

Miriam Therese Winter, *God-With-Us:
Resources for Prayer and Praise* (Nashville:
Abingdon, 1979). Used by permission.

The Desert blossoms

A devastating fire has turned homes into a wilderness.

What is needed to make this couple's desert blossom?

Mark Edward Harris, *Oakland Fire*, Los Angeles, California. © Mark Edward Harris. Used by permission.

The wilderness and the dry land shall be glad, the desert shall rejoice and blossom; like the crocus it shall blossom abundantly. Say to those who are of a fearful heart, "Be strong, do not fear! Here is your God. God will come with vengeance, with terrible recompense. God will come and save you."

Isaiah 35:1–2a, 4

Wilderness

Leader: **There are many kinds of wilderness.**

Group 1: *Empty, desolate land can be wilderness.*

Group 2: Dangerous city streets can be wilderness.

Group 1: *Lonely times of self-examination can be wilderness.*

Group 2: Crowded places can be wilderness.

Leader: **There are many kinds of deserts.**

Group 1: *Rolling sand without water causes thirst.*

Group 2: Lonely times without anyone listening cause thirst.

Group 1: *Oppression without justice causes thirst.*

Group 2: Regret without forgiveness causes thirst.

Leader: **God brings peace to fearful hearts.**

Group 1: *Finding others with similar fears can encourage us.*

Group 2: Naming a fear can give us the courage to face it.

Group 1: *Acting in the face of fear can free us from its paralysis.*

Group 2: Praying in times of fear can remind us that God is with us.

Leader: **God transforms wilderness.**

Group 1: *A pathway can turn wilderness into a park.*

Group 2: People working together can turn city streets into their home.

Group 1: *A caring touch can turn lonely times into meaningful ones.*

Group 2: Friends can turn crowded places into celebrations.

Leader: **God brings fresh water to the desert.**

Group 1: *Flowers bloom in thirsty lands.*

Group 2: God's love reaches into every loneliness.

Group 1: *Justice comes when people join to resist oppression.*

Group 2: God's forgiveness refreshes human life.

All: **Let us celebrate God's restoring and saving power! Amen.**

Life in the Wilderness

Joy Shall Come

Hebrew Melody

Joy shall come e-ven to the wild-er-ness
And the parched land shall then know great glad-ness;
As the rose, as the rose shall des-erts blos-som,
Des-erts like a gar-den blos-som. For liv-ing springs
shall give cool wa-ter, in the des-ert
streams shall flow, For liv-ing springs
shall give cool wa-ter, in the des-ert streams shall flow.

NAME THE CHILD

EMMANUEL

O Come, O Come, Emmanuel

O come, O come, Emmanuel,
And ransom captive Israel,
That mourns in lonely exile here,
Until the Child of God appear.
Rejoice! Rejoice!
Emmanuel shall come to you,
O Israel!

O come, O Wisdom from on high,
And order all things far and nigh;
To us the path of knowledge show,
And help us in that way to go.
Rejoice! Rejoice!
Emmanuel shall come to you,
O Israel!

. . .

O come, O Day-spring, come and cheer
Our spirits by your advent here;
Love stir within the womb of night,
And death's own shadows put to flight.
Rejoice! Rejoice!
Emmanuel shall come to you,
O Israel!

O come, Desire of Nations, bind
All peoples in one heart and mind;
Make envy, strife, and quarrels cease;
Fill the whole world with heaven's peace.
Rejoice! Rejoice!
Emmanuel shall come to you,
O Israel!

Latin c. 9th century, trans. John M. Neale,
1851; sts. 1, 4 trans. Henry S. Coffin, 1916, alt.;
in *The New Century Hymnal* (Cleveland, Ohio:
The Pilgrim Press, 1995), 116.

She will bear a son, and you are to name him Jesus, for Jesus will save the people from their sins. All this took place to fulfill what had been spoken by God through the prophet: "Look, the virgin shall conceive and bear a son, and they shall name him Emmanuel," which means, "God is with us."

Matthew 1:21–23

Aminah Brenda Lynn Robinson, *What You Gonna Name That Pretty Little Baby?*
from *The Teachings: Drawn from African-American Spirituals* (Orlando: Harcourt,
Brace, Jovanovich, 1992). © 1992 by Aminah Brenda Lynn Robinson.
Reprinted by permission of Harcourt, Brace and Company.

We are called to proclaim the truth. . . . And let us believe:

It is not true that this world and its people are doomed to die and be lost.

This is true: I have come that they may have life in all its abundance.

It is not true that we must accept inhumanity and discrimination, hunger and poverty, death and destruction.

This is true: the deaf hear, the dead are raised to life, the poor are hearing the good news.

It is not true that violence and hatred should have the last word, and that war and destruction have come to stay forever.

This is true: death shall be no more, neither shall there be mourning nor crying nor pain anymore.

It is not true that we are simply victims of the powers of evil who seek to rule the world.

This is true: the Lord whom we seek will suddenly come to the temple; and the Lord is like a refiner's fire.

It is not true that our dreams of liberation, of human dignity, are not meant for this earth and for this history.

This is true: it is already time for us to wake from sleep. For the night is far gone, the day is at hand.

Allan Boesak, adapted from an address for the World Council of Churches in *Bread of Tomorrow*, ed. Janet Morley (Maryknoll, N.Y.: Orbis Press, 1992), 31. Used by permission.

Aminah Brenda Lynn Robinson, *What You Gonna Name That Pretty Little Baby?* from *The Teachings: Drawn from African-American Spirituals*, detail, (Orlando: Harcourt, Brace, Jovanovich, 1992). © 1992 by Aminah Brenda Lynn Robinson. Reprinted by permission of Harcourt, Brace and Company.

O come, Emmanuel.

O come, Wisdom.

O come, Day-Spring.

O come, Desire of Nations.

Proclaim THe TRUTH

Gloria in Excelsis Deo

Praise God! Praise God
from the heavens;
praise God in the heights!
Praise God, all God's angels;
praise God, all God's host!
Young men and women alike,
old and young together!
Let them praise the name
of God for God's name
alone is exalted!

Psalm 148:1–2, 12–13a

Mark Wyland, *Whaling Wall VI: Hawaiian Humpbacks*, Laguna Beach, California.
Used by permission.

Picture yourself on the scaffolding next to an animal the size of this whale.
What do you feel? Awe? Fear? Humility?
When we worship on Christmas Eve and Christmas Day,
we are praising the One who appeared as a newborn, helpless baby.
A week later we are praising the same God for creating such great, powerful creatures as whales.
Do you have a sense of awe at the infinite expanse and variety of God's creative powers?

God of the Sparrow
God of the Whale

Words: Jaroslav J. Vajda

Music: Carl F. Schalk

1. God	of	the	spar - row	God	of	the	whale
2. God	of	the	earth - quake	God	of	the	storm
3. God	of	the	rain - bow	God	of	the	cross
4. God	of	the	hun - gry	God	of	the	sick
5. God	of	the	neigh - bor	God	of	the	foe
6. God	of	the	a - ges	God	near	at	hand

God	of	the	swirl - ing	stars
God	of	the	trum - pet	blast
God	of	the	emp - ty	grave
God	of	the	prod - i - gal	
God	of	the	prun - ing	hook
God	of	the	lov - ing	heart

How	does	the	crea - ture	say	Awe
How	does	the	crea - ture	cry	Woe
How	does	the	crea - ture	say	Grace
How	does	the	crea - ture	say	Care
How	does	the	crea - ture	say	Love
How	do	your	chil - dren	say	Joy

1-5 / 6

How	does	the	crea - ture	say	Praise
How	does	the	crea - ture	cry	Save
How	does	the	crea - ture	say	Thanks
How	does	the	crea - ture	say	Life
How	does	the	crea - ture	say	Peace
How	do	your	chil - dren	say	Home

How *does* the creature?

In the space below,
create a poem
or write a paragraph
that offers your
own answers to the
questions at the
end of each verse
of the hymn.

GOD

in the Flesh

And the Word became flesh and dwelt among us, full of grace and truth.

John 1:14a

She holds the baby up

in admiration and with joy.

This baby, her flesh

and blood, is Jesus

the Savior.

Emil Nolde, *Holy Night*, Stiftung Seebull Emil und Ada Nolde, Neukirchen, Germany. Used by permission.

Christmas Litany

In the beginning was the Word,
and the Word was with God

and the Word was God.

In the beginning there was not light,

but the light of God shone in the shadows.

God was the true light.

**Jesus Christ, the Child of God,
came as the light of the world.**

In the beginning was the Word,

and the Word dwelt among us.

All: The Word became flesh full of grace and truth.

Paraphrase of John 1:1, 5, 14

43

Christmas

There are those last exciting, breathtaking hours before Christmas arrives when everything seems to be in its place—the tree, the gifts, the food—all life seems to pause. If you have ever traveled on December 24 you may have noticed how the lights in houses along the way start to appear about twilight. You may have noticed some homes seem busy; others appear quiet.

Each person approaches and experiences Christmas in a different way. Some of us like the noise and colors of the season; others prefer quiet talks with friends—but all of us are usually keenly aware of the expectation.

Then, just like blowing out birthday candles, it is over in a second. Over the next few hours and days life slips back to a normal pace.

Christmas isn't really a "once and done" thing, you know. Christmas is a way of life. In the Gospel of John it says that at the moment of the birth of Jesus, God's Word became flesh and stayed to live with us. This year let's hold over Christmas by popular demand—let's keep it in our hearts.

God Plays NO Favorites

Another Miracle

Then Peter began to speak to them: "I truly understand that God shows no partiality, but in every nation anyone who fears God and does what is right is acceptable to God. You know the message God sent to the people of Israel, preaching peace by Jesus Christ—Christ is Lord of all."

Acts 10:34–36

God, it's a miracle—
>Maybe even more amazing than sunrise and sunset,

Maybe more incredible than the atomic structure of the universe,
>Or the commanding sweep of an eagle's wing,

Maybe more than my extraordinary life, even—
>Sure: your whole creation is miraculous!

But here's another one—an almost inconceivable miracle:
>That you don't play favorites!

Really—how do you do that?
>How do you keep from being partial to

One side or the other one nation over others one team over
>another one race over others one school over another or one

Ice cream flavor over another one brother over another brother one sister over
>another sister one candidate over another or one church over another, even!

Really—how do you stay impartial?
>Don't you read the ads, watch the 6:00 news,

>go to the games, listen to the campaign speeches?

If you did, you'd know the best person, best product, best team, best everything!
>But—I guess you already know what's best, right?

And what's right is best, I guess. And that's not being partial, it's just
>Being good…being God.

If we could all be as impartial as you, that would be a miracle!
>Meanwhile, God, if you want to know about another kind of miracle,

Try the newest flavor of Jen and Harry's ice cream. Yum!
>You just may change your mind about not having any favorites!

Deborah Rose

Cartoonist Charles Schultz gets us to look at many human traits and foibles through the characters he has created in *Peanuts*. What human trait is Snoopy revealing to us? We may assume that we are God's favored creatures. It is also common to think in terms of one's own nation, race, social group, school, or team as "most favored." Who gets to decide?

If you like, write a personal reflection on "favoritism." What are its hazards? Can you offer an example?

Charles Schulz, as reproduced in *The Gospel According to Peanuts* (Glasgow, Scotland: M. E. Bratcher), 114. Used by permission of United Feature Syndicate, Inc.

Dear God, help us become more accepting of one another and all people.

Bill Watterson, as reproduced in *Attack of the Deranged Mutant Killer Monster Snow Goons*, © 1992 by Bill Watterson. Used by permission of Universal Press Syndicate, Inc.

Have you ever felt like Calvin? Does it seem to you that some people get away with a lot more than others? Why do you think God doesn't send lightning bolts or some other form of punishment? Does it seem that God is playing favorites in that instance?

Perhaps you'd like to write a letter of praise or criticism to God, presenting your views on God's impartiality.

What
Are You Seeking?

The next day John again was standing with two of his disciples, and as he watched Jesus walk by, he exclaimed, "Look, here is the Lamb of God!" The two disciples heard him say this, and they followed Jesus. When Jesus turned and saw them following, he said to them, "What are you looking for?"

John 1:35–38a

Little Lamb

Little Lamb, who made thee?
Dost thou know who made thee?
Gave thee life and bid thee feed,
By the stream & o'er the mead;
Gave thee clothing of delight,
Softest clothing wooly bright;
Gave thee such a tender voice,
Making all the vales rejoice!
Little Lamb who made thee?
Dost thou know who made thee?

Little Lamb I'll tell thee,
Little Lamb I'll tell thee!
He is callèd by thy name,
For he calls himself a Lamb:
He is meek & he is mild,
He became a little child:
I a child & thou a lamb
We are callèd by his name.
Little Lamb God bless thee.
Little Lamb God bless thee.

William Blake, "The Lamb,"
in *Poetry and Prose of William Blake*
(New York: Doubleday, 1965), 8–9.

Ethan Hubbard, *Young Herdsman, Peru,* as reproduced in *Straight to the Heart: Children of the World* (Chelsea, Vt.: Craftsbury Common Books). Used by permission.

Look at how gentle the boy is with his flock and how one turns toward him. Jesus is portrayed in Scripture as both Lamb and Good Shepherd.

Can you identify the three different lambs to which the poet refers? Find the lines that are repeated. Which lamb(s) is the poet addressing?

Jan van Eyck, *The Ghent Altarpiece*, 1432, Vijd Chapel, Cathedral St. Bravo, Ghent, Belgium (Scala/Art Resource, N.Y.). Used by permission.

In this picture, the lamb, representing Jesus, is an object of worship. The lamb stands on the altar, placidly waiting to be sacrificed. Is this idea strange to you? Is "Lamb of God" a way you think of Jesus? Why or why not? What names for Jesus help you to see him most clearly? Why?

Lamb of God

Lamb of God, who takes away the sin of the world, have mercy on us.

Lamb of God, who takes away the sin of the world, have mercy on us.

Lamb of God, who takes away the sin of the world, grant us peace.

Read the poem carefully. The poet assumes her readers will recognize the Lamb of God imagery. Is her feeling about God and Jesus similar to or different from the painter Jan van Eyck's in *The Ghent Altarpiece*? Give reasons for your answer. How does the poem make you feel? Do you find any lines especially powerful? Troublesome? Touching? Thought-provoking?

God then,
encompassing all things, is
defenseless? Omnipotence
has been tossed away, reduced
to a wisp of damp wool?

And we,
    frightened, bored, wanting
only to sleep till catastrophe
has raged, clashed, seethed and gone
    by without us, wanting then
to awaken in quietude without
    remembrance of agony,

we who in shamefaced private hope
had looked to be plucked from fire and given
a bliss we deserved for having imagined it,

is it implied that we
must protect this perversely weak
animal, whose muzzle's nudgings
suppose there is milk to be found in us?
Must hold to our icy hearts
a shivering God?

So be it.
    Come, rag of pungent
quiverings,
    dim start
        Let's try
if something human still
can shield you,
        spark
of remote light.

Denise Levertov, "Mass for the Day of St. Thomas Didymus" (excerpt), in *Candles in Babylon* (New York: New Directions, 1982). Used by permission.

TRUST in God

God is my light and my salvation; whom shall I fear? God is the stronghold of my life; of whom shall I be afraid?

Psalm 27:1

David F. Johnson,
Ellie and Raymond,
New York, New York.
Used by permission.

Do you know anyone with AIDS or another life-threatening disease? Did your feelings toward that person change when you found out that he or she was sick? Do you know if he or she is afraid? If you claim God as your stronghold, does that help you reach out to someone who may be frightened—of AIDS or anything else? Consider ways that you may take light into the shadows for someone who is afraid.

Take light into the shadows.

WHOM SHALL I FEAR?

I shall not fear _____ (name a person or group).

God is my salvation.

I shall not fear _____ (a disease or illness).

God is my strength.

I will not fear _____ (a disaster).

God is the stronghold of my life.

I will not fear destruction, disease, or devastation,

For God is my light.

I shall not fear. I shall _not_ fear.

Christian singer-songwriter Amy Grant wrote the lyrics to this, one of her most popular songs. Her fans bring lighters to her concerts, and during the song, they hold them high above their heads, swaying to the music as she sings. The shadows of an amphitheater are transformed by hundreds of dancing lights.

Whenever you feel afraid, especially at night, consider lighting a candle to remind you that God is at your side. You could even say or sing this song or memorize today's scripture (Psalm 27:1).

Thy Word Is a Lamp

Thy word is a lamp unto my feet
   and a light unto my path.
When I feel afraid,
think I've lost my way,
still you're there right beside me,
and nothing will I fear as long
   as you are near.
Please be near me to the end.
Thy word is a lamp unto my feet
   and a light unto my path.
Now I will not forget your love
   for me
and yet my heart forever is
   wandering.
Jesus, be my guide and hold me
   to your side,
and I will love you to the end.

what God requires

Maerten van Heemskerck, *Tobit Burying the Dead, Feeding the Poor and Visiting Prisoners*, private collection.

God has told you, O mortal, what is good; and what does God require of you but to do justice, and to love kindness, and to walk humbly with your God?

Micah 6:8

This picture, which was created during the Renaissance, shows a man by the name of Tobit welcoming the sick, hungry, and deprived people of his time. There is a child standing near Tobit with his arm outstretched holding an empty bowl. The other people that approach Tobit have solemn, joyless expressions on their faces and some appear to be in physical pain. Tobit welcomes them—he reaches out to touch the head of an ailing man in front of him. Where are you in this picture? Are you the hungry child, the ailing man, someone else in line, Tobit, the gravedigger, or a bystander?

Called as Partners
In Christ's Service

Called as partners in Christ's service,
Called to ministries of grace,
We respond with deep commitment
Fresh new lines of faith to trace.
May we learn the art of sharing,
Side by side and friend with friend,
Equal partners in our caring
To fulfill God's chosen end.

prayer

God, Creator and Sustainer, help us to fight for justice. Give us courage to speak out for those who are hurt and oppressed. Give us the strength and the imagination to show kindness to all creatures. Keep us from turning our backs on those who need our help and are eager for any kind of gesture we can give. Help us to live up to your expectations and walk humbly by your side. Amen.

If I Have Been the Source of Pain

If I have been the source of pain, O God;
If to the weak I have refused my strength;
If, in rebellion, I have strayed away;
Forgive me, God.

If I have spoken words of cruelty;
If I have left some suffering unrelieved;
Condemn not my insensitivity;
Forgive me, God.

If I've insisted on a peaceful life,
Far from the struggles that the gospel brings,
When you prefer to guide me to the strife,
Forgive me, God.

Receive, O God, this ardent word of prayer,
And free me from temptation's subtle snare,
With tender patience, lead me to your care.
Amen, Amen.

Sara M. de Hall, "Si Fui Motivo de Dolor, Oh Dios (If I Have Been the Source of Pain, O God)," based on a text by C. M. Battersby, trans. Janet W. May, in *The New Century Hymnal* (Cleveland, Ohio: The Pilgrim Press, 1995). English translation copyright © 1992 United Church Board for Homeland Ministries/The Pilgrim Press, Cleveland, Ohio. Used by permission.

Shine!

Kim Woong, *The Coming of the Light*, as reproduced in Masao Takenaka, ed., *Christian Art in Asia* (Tokyo: Kyo Bun Kwan in association with the Asian Christian Art Association, 1975), 148. Used by permission of the Asian Christian Art Association.

The artist Kim Woong has painted a picture of a young person grasping a candle in the midst of shadows. Look at the posture and the expression on her face. What does the title *The Coming of the Light* suggest to you?

Let your light shine before others.

Matthew 5:16b

Litany

Light one candle.
Light one candle in a shadowy space.
Light one candle, and then one more.
Two lit candles, then three or four.
Light the candles, fill the night.
Light the candles, fill the day.
Burning candles start a glow.
Burning candles in a row.
Christ the promise.
Christ the light.
Christ says let your light shine.
Christ says my light is thine.
All: Let your light shine before others.

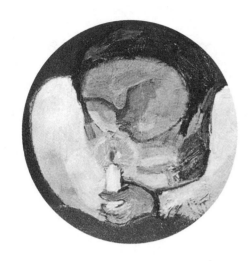

Based on her posture, how important do you think the candle is to this person? What does she have to do to let this light shine?

This Little Light of Mine

This little light of mine,

I'm gonna let it shine.

This little light of mine,

I'm gonna let it shine.

This little light of mine.

I'm gonna let it shine.

Let it shine, let it shine, let it shine.

African American Traditional

Your First Candle

On your first birthday you probably had a birthday cake with one candle. Maybe you even have a photograph that shows you blowing it out. Each year in everyone's life more candles are added to the birthday cake. As we grow older the light from our birthday cake grows brighter and brighter.

In some churches the parents and sponsors of a baby are handed a lighted candle when an infant is baptized. The candle is given as a symbol of the light of Christ being passed on to the newest member of the Christian family.

Picture yourself as you are today standing in your church at the place where baptisms are performed. Think for a moment about a lighted candle being handed to you. As you reach to accept it a quiet voice says, "Let your light shine!"

growing in God

Rex Goreleigh, *Planting*, Evans-Tibbs Collection of Afro-American Art, Washington, D.C. Used by permission.

What then is Apollos? What is Paul? Servants through whom you came to believe, as the Lord assigned to each. I planted, Apollos watered, but only God gave the growth. So neither the one who plants nor the one who waters is anything, but only God who gives the growth.

1 Corinthians 3:5–7

Litany

Gently the great hand of God places the seed.

The seed of faith.

Gently the seed of faith becomes a sprout.

The seedling of faith.

God encourages it to grow.

The tiny faith expands.

God nurtures the new life.

The growing faith takes shape.

Gently God showers it with love.

The faith and soul stir.

Gently God sends strength and endurance.

The faith and soul become one spirit,

All: Growing in God.

You can almost feel the effort it takes this person to bend down and plant this seedling. Those massive hands gently position the thin twig. The whole person is so large and sturdy compared to the tiny thing between her fingers. Those hands or feet could just as easily crush as nurture. Have you ever planted a seed and tended the new sprout? How tender and fragile new life can be. Faith is the seed God plants in our hearts; how tender and fragile that new faith can be!

This is a Native American hymn that praises the many and great works of God. The words include insights into the power of God to create and sustain life. As you read the verses, visualize God at work in the universe and in your heart.

God is the gardener.

Be a gardener.
Dig a ditch,
toil and sweat,
and turn the earth upside down
and seek the deepness
and water the plants in time.
Continue this labor
and make sweet floods to run
and noble and abundant fruits
to spring.
Take this food and drink
and carry it to God
as your true worship.

Julian of Norwich, *Meditations with Julian of Norwich*, ed. Brendan Doyle (Santa Fe: Bear and Co., 1983). Used by permission.

Wakantanka Taku Nitawa
Many and Great, O God, Are Your Works

Many and great, O God, are your works,
  Maker of earth and sky;
Your hands have set the heavens with stars,
  Your fingers spread the mountains and plains.
Lo, at your word the waters were formed;
  Deep seas obey your voice.

Grant unto us communion with you,
  O star abiding One;
Come unto us and dwell with us:
  With you are found the gifts of life.
Bless us with life that has no end,
  Eternal life with you.

Joseph R. Renville, paraphrased by R. Philip Frazier. in *The New Century Hymnal* (Cleveland, Ohio: The Pilgrim Press, 1995).

dear God, our Creator and Redeemer, thank you for the seed of faith that has been planted in our hearts. Help us to let it grow and to understand that it is your power that nurtures and sustains it. Be with us always and bless our growing. Amen.

We Were *Witnesses*

For we did not follow cleverly devised myths when we made known to you the power and coming of Christ Jesus, but we had been eyewitnesses of Jesus' majesty. For Jesus received honor and glory from God when that voice was conveyed by the Majestic Glory, saying, "This is my child, my Beloved, with whom I am well pleased." We ourselves heard this voice come from heaven, while we were with Jesus on the holy mountain.

2 Peter 1:16–18

David C. Driskell, Movement, *The Mountain*, Evans-Tibbs Collection of Afro-American Art, Washington, D.C. Used by permission.

Litany

Come, Jesus, come to us.
Come Beloved Child of God.
Come to our hearts and minds,
that we might be transformed.
Come, Jesus,
claim our hearts,
Move us to new understanding,
and to new life in Christ.
Come, Jesus,
Come to us.

A voice came from God that declared Jesus to be the Beloved and Jesus was transfigured.
The artist David C. Driskell has captured an image of light and shadow that gives one impression of a moment of transfiguration. You, too, can create in your own mind a picture of what the glory of God might look like at the moment God declared that Jesus is the Christ. How does your imagination picture the moment?

PRAYER

Christ, our Redeemer and Savior,
fill our hearts with love so that
we are forever transformed.
Claim our lives so that we may
live in perfect harmony with all
living things. Keep us focused on
a life of service, commitment,
and Christian love. Amen.

The Transfiguration, Vie de Jesus Mafa,
24 rue du Marechal, Joffre, 78000 Versailles,
France. Used by permission.

The Greek *Chi* (X) and *Rho* (P) when placed together become the symbol for Christ. Look for this symbol on the paraments and/or banners of your church.

**Celebrate the glory
and majesty of Christ
that claims and
transforms lives.**

Christ enters our lives when _____.

To be transformed by Christ means _____.

Christ claims our lives by _____.

As a person claimed by Christ I am called to _____.

TEMPTED

God said, "You shall not eat of the fruit of the tree that is in the middle of the garden, nor shall you touch it, or you shall die." But the serpent said to the woman, "You will not die; for God knows that when you eat of it your eyes will be opened, and you will be like God, knowing good and evil."

Genesis 3:3–5

Michelangelo Buonarotti, *Original Sin and Expulsion from Paradise (Fall of Man)*, 1510, Sistine Chapel, Vatican Palace, Vatican City (Scala/Art Resource, N.Y.). Used by permission.

Does this painting tell a different story than the one in Genesis? What choices do Eve and Adam face? How does the painting inspire you, make you uncomfortable, or move you?

WHICH DOOR TO OPEN?

"What's best and worst?"
        Atkin asked, casually.

"Best makes us long-term happy,
        worst makes us long-term sorry."

"How long-term?"

"Years. A lifetime."

Richard Bach, *One* (New York: Dell, 1988), 121.

GOD, you don't always give us answers when we ask. Perhaps we should be honored that you trust us enough to work out our own solutions. But sometimes it's hard to know what to do. We're faced with so many choices every day. Help us to be able to make good decisions. We know that some decisions lead us down a path that's just more difficult for us. And some decisions open doors for us that lead us to a deeper kind of happiness. Help us to make the choices that might not always be popular, but that lead us closer to you. Thanks most of all for being with us even when we're on the wrong path, even when we make the same mistakes again and again. Amen.

BORN FROM Above

Now there was a Pharisee named Nicodemus, a leader of the Jews. He came to Jesus by night and said, "Rabbi, we know that you are a teacher who has come from God for no one can do these signs that you do apart from the presence of God." Jesus answered him, "Very truly, I tell you, no one can see the dominion of God without being born from above."

John 3:1–3

Eero Saarinen and Associates, architects, *Kresge Chapel at MIT*.
Used by permission of the MIT Museum.

How would you feel if you were in this building on a sunny day, looking up at the skylight? Imagine standing with the sun's rays beaming down on you.

God gives new life; you are born from above.

Create in Me a Clean Heart, O God

Create in me a clean heart, O God,

    and renew a right spirit within me.

Cast me not away from your presence,

    and take not your Holy Spirit from me.

Restore in me the joy of salvation,

    and uphold me with your free spirit.

© Copyright 1991 Emma Lou Diemer.
Used by permission.

John LaFarge, *Visit of Nicodemus to Christ*, gift of William T. Evans,
National Museum of American Art, Smithsonian Institution,
Washington, D.C. Used by permission.

Dear God,

    I know all about where babies come from, I think. From inside mommies, and daddies put them there. Where are they before that? Do you have them in heaven? How do they get here? Do you have to take care of them all first? Please answer all my questions. I always think of you.

Yours truly,

Susan

Stuart Hample and Eric Marshall, *Children's Letters to God: The New Collection*
(New York: Workman Publishing, 1991), 34. Used by permission.

Please answer all my questions.
I always think of you.

Living Water

A Samaritan woman came to draw water, and Jesus said to her, "Give me a drink." (The disciples had gone to the city to buy food.) The Samaritan woman said to Jesus, "How is it that you, a Jew, ask a drink of me, a woman of Samaria?" (Jews do not share things in common with Samaritans.) Jesus answered her, "If you knew the gift of God, and who it is that is saying to you, 'Give me a drink,' you would have asked that one, who would then have given you living water."

John 4:7–10

Jesus and the Samaritan Woman, Catacomb of via Latina. Rome, Italy (Scala/Art Resource, N.Y.). Used by permission.

Tell the story that you see in the painting.
What happens next?

Come to the water.

The history of God's people is filled with stories of living water.

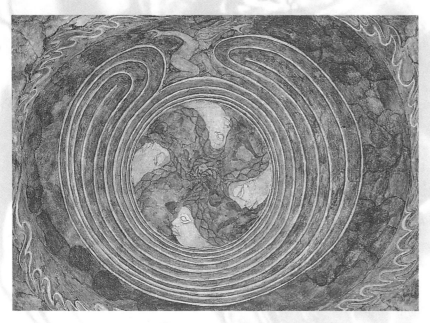

Meinrad Craighead, *Changing Woman*, 1982, ink on scrathboard,
as reproduced in *The Mother's Songs* (Mahwah, N.J.: Paulist Press, 1986), 32.
© Meinrad Craighead. Collection of Myrna Little, Texas.
Used by permission of the artist.

If you look closely at this art, what do you see?

Keep looking. What images from the baptism prayer

can you find in the drawing?

We thank you, God, for the
gift of creation
called forth by your saving Word.
Before the world had shape and form,
your Spirit moved over the waters.
Out of the waters of the deep,
you formed the firmament
and brought forth the earth
to sustain all life.
In the time of Noah,
you washed the earth
with the waters of the flood,
and your ark of salvation bore a
new beginning.
In the time of Moses,
your people Israel passed
through the Red Sea waters
from slavery to freedom
and crossed the flowing Jordan
to enter the promised land.
In the fullness of time,
you sent Jesus Christ,
who was nurtured
in the water of Mary's womb.
Jesus was baptized by John
in the water of the Jordan,
became living water to a woman
at the Samaritan well,
washed the feet of the disciples,
and sent them forth
to baptize all the nations
by water and the Holy Spirit.
By your Holy Spirit
save those who confess
the name of Jesus Christ
that sin may have no power over us.
Create new life in each of us
this day
that we may rise in Christ.
Glory to you, eternal God,
the one who was, and is,
and shall always be,
world without end.
Amen.

United Church of Christ, *Book of Worship*
(New York: United Church of Christ Office for
Church Life and Leadership, 1986), 141–42,
adapted. Used by permission.

That We May Believe

Then the Pharisees also began to ask the man who had been blind how he had received his sight. He said to them, "Jesus put mud on my eyes. Then I washed, and now I see." Some of the Pharisees said, "This man is not from God, for he does not observe the sabbath." But others said, "How can a man who is a sinner perform such signs?" And they were divided. So they said again to the man who had been blind, "What do you say about Jesus? It was your eyes he opened."

John 9:15–17b

Amazing Grace

Amazing grace! How sweet the sound
That saved a wretch like me!
I once was lost but now am found.
Was blind but now I see.

John Newton

Elijah Pierce, *The Man That Was Born Blind Restored to Sight*, 1930, carved and painted wood relief, Michael and Julie Hall Collection of American Folk Art, Milwaukee Art Museum, Wisconsin. Used by permission.

We walked down the path to the well-house, attracted by the fragrance of the honeysuckle with which it was covered. Someone was drawing water and my teacher placed my hand under the spout. As the cool stream gushed over one hand she spelled into the other the word water, first slowly, then rapidly. I stood still, my whole attention fixed upon the motions of her fingers. Suddenly I felt a misty consciousness as of something forgotten—a thrill of returning thought; and somehow the mystery of language was revealed to me. I knew then that "w-a-t-e-r" meant the wonderful cool something that was flowing over my hand. That living word awakened my soul, gave it light, hope, joy, set it free! There were barriers still, it is true, but barriers that could in time be swept away.

I left the well-house eager to learn. Everything had a name, and each name gave birth to a new thought. As we returned to the house every object which I touched seemed to quiver with life. That was because I saw everything with the strange, new sight that had come to me. . . . I learned a great many new words that day. I do not remember what they all were; but I do know that *mother, father, sister, teacher* were among them—words that were to make the world blossom for me, "like Aaron's rod, with flowers." It would have been difficult to find a happier child than I was as I lay in my crib at the close of that eventful day and lived over the joys it had brought me, and for the first time longed for a new day to come.

Helen Keller, *The Story of My Life* (New York: Doubleday, Page and Co., 1903), 23–24.

Can These Bones Live?

David Hiser, *Day of the Dead Celebrations*, Tony Stone Images. Used by permission.

The hand of God came upon me, and God brought me out by the spirit of God and set me down in the middle of a valley; it was full of bones. God said to me, "Mortal, can these bones live? I will lay sinews on you, and will cause flesh to come upon you, and cover you with skin, and put breath in you, and you shall live; and you shall know that I am God."

Ezekiel 37:1–3b, 6

What do you think this photo is about?
Write a caption for it.

A Sign of Hope
in a Valley of Dry
Bones

Chronically plagued by drought, disease, and devastating poverty, Haiti is the poorest country in this hemisphere. Seeing the people and animals, skin-and-bone hungry and dehydrated, I remarked to one of the others on our mission trip there, "This is a valley of dry bones."

Yet that same day, in a small hospital for children in Port au Prince, the cheerful director, Gladys Sylvestre, was encouraging a tiny girl named Jeanette as she was taking her very first steps—at age three and a half. The child's sandals were scuffed hand-me-downs, as was her dress. Much of her hair had fallen out, from malnutrition. Yet her enormous brown eyes were bright as she beamed up at us, thrilled with the adventure and accomplishment of learning to walk.

Gladys told us she had discovered Jeanette several months before, abandoned as hopelessly ill and left to die in the city's General Hospital. "Something about her just made me stop and notice. She called out for me to help her, and I couldn't just leave her there." So Gladys arranged for the little girl to come home with her, and in the weeks to follow, Jeanette underwent surgery and rehabilitation. The day we met her she was vibrant, holding onto Gladys' hand and taking wobbly but determined steps on fragile bones across the nursery floor.

Enjoying our smiles and applause for her achievement, she began swaying, bobbing her head back and forth, all the while grinning at us to beat the band! Gladys laughed and spoke to Jeanette in Creole, who answered, "M'ap danse ak bondye!"

I said, "Would you translate?"

Jeanette's rescuer smiled. "I asked her, 'Jeanette, are you dancing?' She said, 'I'm dancing with God!'"

In the valley, dry bones lived again.

Deborah Grant Rose

Can these bones live?

Your Reflection

Write your own version of the good news of hope in this space. You might consider these questions in your reflection: What do you hope for? Or what makes you hopeful? When has God given you life and hope? Or describe a time when you felt like dry bones being revitalized.

blessed
is the One

The artist of this picture was the son of a poor shepherd in thirteenth-century Italy. Although he lacked the technical knowledge of anatomy and perspective of later Renaissance painters, he expressed human emotion and the significance of events with great sensitivity. Notice the various gestures of adoration among the crowd and the benign expression on the donkey's face. Do you see the children in trees, gathering branches to wave? Besides the large religious frescoes (murals painted on wet plaster) that Giotto painted on the walls of Italian churches, he also designed buildings so beautifully that he was made the city architect of Florence.

When they had come near Jerusalem and had reached Bethphage at the Mount of Olives, Jesus sent two disciples, saying to them, "Go into the village ahead of you, and immediately you will find a donkey tied, and a colt with it; untie them and bring them to me." The crowds that went ahead of Jesus and that followed were shouting, "Hosanna to the Son of David! Blessed is the one who comes in the name of God! Hosanna in the highest heaven!"

Matthew 21:1–2, 9

Giotto, *Entry into Jerusalem*, Scrovegni Chapel, Padua, Italy (Scala/Art Resource, N.Y.). Used by permission.

José Faustino Altamirano, *Blessed Is He*, as reproduced in Philip and Sally Scharper, eds., *The Gospel in Art by the Peasants of Solentiname* (Maryknoll, N.Y.: Orbis Books). Used by permission of Verlagsleiter, Peter Hammer Verlag, Germany.

Peasant art, like folk songs, springs from the "grassroots" of a community. Also like folk songs, the art of peasants is often a form of protest. Sometimes the protest is open, but more often it is subtle, for fear that whoever is in power will crush them for singing or painting their views about the tyranny under which they live. In countries like Nicaragua, where this painting was made, many people possess—if little else—a vibrant faith in Christ as their liberator. Do you find in this picture any indication of political protest by the peasants of Solentiname?

Prayer for Holy Week

Dear God, we thank you for Jesus, who was your obedient servant and servant of humankind. Help us follow his example of humble servanthood. And yet we also accept Jesus as the Christ, most sovereign of sovereigns, who reigns with you through eternity. Help us accept Christ's reign over our lives. Thank you for being with us in the triumphant days of our lives, as well as in the lonely nights. Thank you for being with us when we suffer, when we're on trial, and when we're betrayed. Thank you for holy days, for holy weeks, and for the promise of Easter morning.

Amen.

Go & Tell

The angel said, "Do not be afraid;
I know that you are looking for Jesus
who was crucified. Jesus is not here;
but has been raised, as Jesus said.
Come, see the place where Jesus lay.
Then go quickly and tell the disciples,
'Jesus has been raised from the dead,
and indeed is going ahead of you to
Galilee; there you will see Jesus.'
This is my message for you."

Matthew 28:5b–7

A Traditional Easter Greeting

One: Christ is risen.

All: Christ is risen indeed!

One: Christ is risen.

All: Christ is risen indeed!

One: Christ is risen.

All: Christ is risen indeed!

One: Alleluia!

All: Alleluia!

One: Amen.

All: Amen.

John Biggers, *The Upper Room*, Artcetra, Houston, Texas. Used by permission.

This is an unusual painting to connect with the Easter morning scene at the empty tomb. What do you recognize of Matthew's Easter story? The artist has included many symbols in the picture; perhaps they might suggest that mystery surrounds the resurrection of Jesus. Can you guess the meaning of some of the symbols?

Go and Tell

Go...but where should I go?

Tell...but what should I say?

Should I say the way it is for me...

That the news is so good I can barely
contain it within myself?

Sometimes it comes to me like a dozen
helium balloons,

and I do nothing but float above everyone
and everything.

I'm soaring!

Sometimes it comes like a quiet assurance.

It doesn't stop me from crying,

It doesn't make the problems go away,

But I know I'm not alone

and I can hear the voice within me,

"It'll be all right."

And sometimes it comes as a song with a
marching beat.

It makes me want to change things,

right the wrongs,

Set up a debate or speak up in class,

Give away soup or go the second mile.

It's good news to me.

I may not share it in those words

but if you ask me

if you listen to me

you'll know it too.

Kelly Boyte Peters

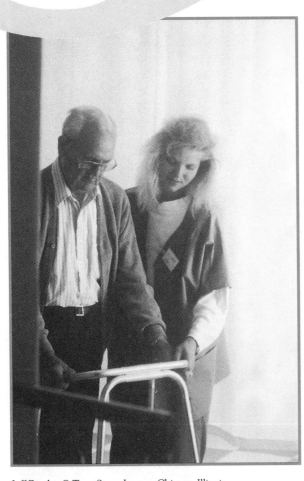

Jeff Zaruba, © Tony Stone Images, Chicago, Illinois.
Used by permission.

Room for doubt

Jesus said to Thomas, "Have you believed because you have seen me? Blessed are those who have not seen and yet have come to believe."

John 20:29

Rembrandt Harmensz van Rijn, *Doubting Thomas*, Pushkin Museum of Fine Arts, Moscow, Russia (Scala/Art Resource N.Y.). Used by permission.

These Things Did Thomas Count as Real

These things did Thomas count as real:
　　The warmth of blood, the chill of steel,
The grain of wood, the heft of stone,
　　The last frail twitch of flesh and bone.

The vision of his skeptic mind
　　Was keen enough to make him blind
To any unexpected act
　　Too large for his small world of fact.

His reasoned certainties denied
　　That one could live when one had died,
Until his fingers read like Braille
　　The markings of the spear and nail.

May we, O God, by grace believe
　　And thus the risen Christ receive,
Whose raw imprinted palms reached out
　　And beckoned Thomas from his doubt

Thomas H. Troeger. Words © Copyright 1984 Oxford University Press. Used by permission.

the artist, Rembrandt Harmensz van Rijn, has effectively used light and shadows to depict the revelation that Jesus is the risen Christ. We see Jesus showing his wounds to Thomas, the disciple who said he would not believe that Jesus was raised from the dead until he could actually touch the wounds inflicted on the cross. Look at the face of Thomas and his posture. What do you think is going through his mind at that moment? For centuries people have confessed a belief in Jesus as the risen Christ without visual proof of his existence. What do you believe?

The Younger Brother of Thomas

Thomas really didn't touch him.
I would have.
What can you prove just by looking?
Since when is seeing believing?
They killed my brother's friend
That's fact.
And Thomas just went crazy.
I was there.
It hurt to hear him cry like that.
I don't want to go crazy like Thomas has.
And then this story starts:
that Jesus isn't dead,
that he's been seen
walking through walls,
showing up at supper time.
But nobody, nobody had touched him.
Thomas didn't buy it.
I wouldn't have either.
Never listen to an eyewitness.
Get the facts firsthand.
Don't settle for someone
you can't get a hold of.
But then this ghost or hoax appeared
and called his name.
Thomas took one look
and thought that he'd seen God.
He really didn't touch him, see.
But doubting Thomas believes.
It would take more than that
to convince me.
Doubting runs in the family.

Heather Murray Elkins, "The Younger Brother of Thomas,"
Accent on Youth 7, no. 2 (Spring 1985): 2.
Used by permission.

Since when is seeing believing?

Serious **doubt** is **confirmation** of faith.

Paul Tillich, *Dynamics of Faith* (New York: Harper, 1957),
22. © Copyright 1957 by Paul Tillich, © Copyright 1985
by Hanna Tillich. Used by permission of HarperCollins
Publishers, Inc.

present at the Table

Then they told what had happened on the road, and how Jesus had been made known to them in the breaking of the bread.

Luke 24:35

litany

Enter our hearts and lives.
Christ, be present.
  Take us safely through tough times.
  Christ, be present.
   Fill us with compassion.
   Christ, be present.
   Take away our fear of others.
   Christ, be present.
   Replace all prejudice with love.
  Christ, be present.
  All: Christ, reveal yourself to us.

Caravaggio, *Supper at Emmaus*, National Gallery of Art, London, England (Nimatallah/Art Resource, N.Y.). Used by permission.

notice how the artist (Italian Renaissance painter Caravaggio) achieves the sense of a highly dramatic moment by his use of sharply contrasting light and shadow. How else does he convey intensity and amazement? Can you identify the characters in the scene? Can you imagine what they are saying? It is a moment of profound revelation for those at the table. When we break bread during Holy Communion, Christ is present at the table.

prayer

Christ our Savior and Redeemer, help us to recognize you at the table, in our lives, and in the faces of other people. Help us to understand what your presence means to each of us. Amen.

Christ at the Table

I have stood with the congregation,
Sipped from the cup,
Tasted the bread.
I have prayed with the congregation,
for Christ to enter
and fill my soul.
I have looked at the faces around me,
plain folk and fancy,
old folk and young.
I have searched for the face of Jesus,
asked when the Christ
would appear.
Have I looked past the face of Jesus?
Have I not seen the Christ in another?
Have I missed him at the table?
I will stand again with the congregation
and look for Christ
in their midst.

imagine what it would be like to walk down a quiet road talking with Jesus. Think about the questions you could ask him. Think about the way he would respond and how his voice might sound.

There are times in most Christians' lives when they are able to feel close to their Savior. The resurrected Christ is still revealed to us today. There are moments during baptism and during Holy Communion when Christ enters the lives of those present. To walk with Christ may mean opening your heart to let Christ's presence enter in. Think about it.

Abundant Life

Day by day, as they spent much time together in the temple, they broke bread at home and ate their food with glad and generous hearts, praising God and having the good will of all people.

Acts 2:46–47a

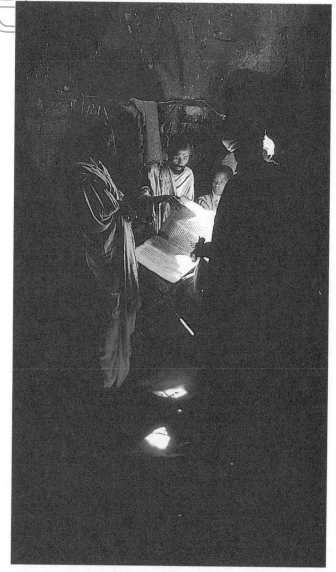

Georg Gerster, *Coptic Church*, © National Geographic Society, Washington, D.C. Used by permission.

The light falls on the open book, a crowd moves close to find out what it says. The Word of God, the message of salvation, is written within its pages. Each page is gently turned; each phrase is read with anticipating heart. The Word of God is within your grasp. The message of salvation, an abundant life and life within the community of believers, is waiting for you.

Litany

Let us break bread together,
Praising God.
Let us eat with glad and generous hearts,
Praising God.
Let us celebrate the abundance of life,
Praising God.
All: Praise God from whom all blessings flow.

Hine Ma Tov
(How Very Good and Pleasant It Is)

Words: Psalm 133:1

Music: Israeli round

Prayer

O God, sustainer of all life, help us to serve you in the community of believers with glad hearts. Let us never forget to praise you for the abundant life that is within our reach. Amen.

May God make your hearts glad and generous.

Quickly, with energy

Part 1

How ver - y good and how plea - sant when kin - dred sit to - geth - er;

Part 2

To dwell as one, how ver - y good it is.

To sing this as a round, divide into two groups. Group A sings part 1 twice, then part 2 twice. Group B sings part 1 as group A sings part 2, and so forth.

Arr. copyright ©1994 by United Church Press.

The early believers gathered at the table, broke bread, and ate their food with glad and generous hearts. They were glad, for they knew that God had showed them the way to an abundant life. That way involved selling their possessions to provide for those who could not afford meals such as this.

The abundant life is achieved by a God who makes *our* hearts generous.

78

God's Own People

Litany

We are a chosen race,

God's own people.

We are a royal priesthood,

God's own people.

We are a holy nation,

God's own people.

Once we were not a people,
but now we are

God's own people.

Once we had not received
mercy, but as

God's own people

All: we have received mercy.

But you are a chosen race, a royal priesthood, a holy nation, God's own people, in order that you may proclaim the mighty acts of the one who called you out of the night into God's marvelous light. Once you were not a people, but now you are God's people; once you had not received mercy, but now you have received mercy.

1 Peter 2:9–10

Arthur Boyd, *Moses Leading the People*, as reproduced in *Images of Religion in Australian Art*, ed. Rosemary Crumlin (Kensington, NSW: Bay Books, 1988), plate 70. Used by permission.

The words of 1 Peter 2 recall God's saving act, Moses and the Exodus. The covenant between God and the people established the Hebrews as God's own. The writer of First Peter identifies the church as a continuation of "the people of God."

John August Swanson, *Festival of Lights*, 1991, acrylic painting on masonite, Bergsma Gallery, Grand Rapids, Michigan. © 1991 John August Swanson. Used by permission.

My People

The night is
beautiful,

So, the face of
my people.

The stars are
beautiful,

So the eyes of my
people.

Beautiful, also,
is the sun.

Beautiful, also,
are the souls of
my people.

Langston Hughes,
"My People," in *Listen,
Children* (New York:
Bantam Books, 1982), 57.
Used by permission of
Alfred A. Knopf.

Prayer

God, our Creator and Redeemer, help us
to build on the cornerstone of our faith in
Jesus Christ and live up to your expectations
as your chosen people. Give us strength,
wisdom, patience, and love. Amen.

The chosen people of God
have built their church on the
cornerstone of Jesus Christ.
You are one of God's chosen!

Because I Live, You Live

Jesus said, "In a little while the world will no longer see me, but you will see me; because I live, you also will live. On that day you will know that I am in God, and you in me, and I in you."

John 14:19–20

Litany

Jesus said,

Soon you will

no longer see me.

Jesus told them,

I will not leave

you desolate.

Jesus assured them,

The Comforter will come.

Jesus promised,

Because I live,

All: You will live also.

Bagong Kussudiardja, *The Ascension*, as reproduced in Masao Takenaka and Ron O'Grady, *The Bible Through Asian Eyes* (Auckland, New Zealand: Pace Publishing in association with The Asian Christian Art Association, 1991), 165. Used by permission of The Asian Christian Art Association.

Look at the motion

of the figure in this picture. What an experience!

The artist shows us Jesus at the moment of the

Ascension, how transformed he appears to be.

What would it feel like to be in his place?

Metamorphosis

What is seen is yet unseen.
I hold a tiny seed that has life,
but does not show it.
That which is within it stirs to be free.
I hold a vision of eternal life,
a life in Christ that is never-ending.
There is a moment when, like Jesus,
I will pass through the unmarked door,
to a new place.
It is the place that holds eternal life.
I hear the voice of one who
        was sent to comfort me.
The Spirit, the Christ, the
        God everlasting,
all three.

Prayer

Jesus, our Savior

and Redeemer,

help us to know

that you are with

us in all that we do.

Give us comfort and

hope. Help us to know

that you live in us.

Amen.

Consider

Consider Statements of Faith

- I know I have life in Christ when _____

- I know the Spirit is with me when _____

- I know that I belong to God when _____

Steadfast in FAITH

Cast all your anxieties on God, because God cares for you.

1 Peter 5:7

LITANY

Give up to God.
Be steadfast in faith.
Give to God all anxieties.
Be steadfast in faith.
Give your fears to the One
who cares for you.
Be steadfast in faith.
I place my fears with God,
I tell God all that troubles me.
God hears my cries,
God takes away my fear.
All: Be steadfast in faith.

Pablo Picasso, *Woman Crying*, Prado, Madrid, Spain (Bridgeman/Art Resource, N.Y.).
© ARS. Used by permission.

One glance at the face of this woman and you know that she has reached the depths of despair. What feelings does the painting bring up for you? What could be her fears and anxieties? Have you ever felt as this woman does? No one needs to feel this way. Give God your anxieties and let God cry with you.

What if you gave all your fears to God. What would be left? What if everyone you met had given their fears to God. What would the world be like?

If we had no fear, we would try many things. We might try sharing God's love with others. We might find that the more we gave away the more we would have to give away again. God is always willing to fill and renew us.

God cares for you. God cares for us. God cares for everyone. What would it be like to give up to God?

Love *Future* *HOME* *School* *Money* *JOB* *WARS* *FAMILY* *Friends* *Grades* *World* *Community*

ALL
ANXIETIES
GO
HERE

**God cares for you. God cares for us.
God cares for everyone.
What would it be like to give up to God?**

O God, our Creator and our Sustainer. Here they are. Here are all our fears. We don't want them anymore; we give them freely to you. You have said it, and we believe it. You care for us and we are your own. Thanks be to God. Amen.

Prayer

Filled
with the Spirit

When the day of Pentecost had come, they were all together in one place. All of them were filled with the Holy Spirit and began to speak in other languages, as the Spirit gave them ability.

Acts 2:1, 4

In what ways do you connect this image with the image of Jesus' followers at Pentecost?

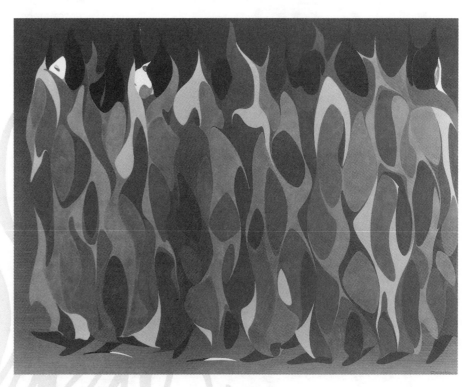

Oscar Howe, *Ghost Dance*, 1960, The Heard Museum, Phoenix, Arizona.
© 1983 by Adelheid Howe. Used by permission.

Veni Sancte Spiritus

Veni Sancte Spiritus.

Veni Sancte Spiritus.

Come, Holy Spirit,

from heaven shine forth

with your glorious light.

Veni Sancte Spiritus.

Words: Come, Holy Spirit, verses drawn from the *Pentecost Sequence*, Taizé Community, 1978.
Used by permission of G.I.A. Publications, Inc., Chicago, Illinois, exclusive agent. All rights reserved.

At Pentecost, Peter and the disciples spoke in many different languages about the good news of Jesus. The following all say "good news." How many languages can you identify?

"Ghost Dancers," Indians of the North American West, were moved by the visions and spiritual hope of a nineteenth-century "crisis cult," which developed in response to their continuing displacement and oppression. Their hope was for the departure of the white settlers, and the restoration of their land and the buffalo. This abstract depiction renders the dancers' characteristic red coats as flames of passion.

Bonnes Nouvelles (French)
Good News **Buenas Noticias (Spanish)**
Buona Notizia (Italian)

What would you do?

Exuberant Spirit of God

Exuberant Spirit of God,
bursting with the brightness of flame
into the coldness of our lives
to warm us with a passion for justice and beauty,
we praise you.

Exuberant Spirit of God,
sweeping us out of the dusty corners of our apathy
to breath vitality into our struggles for change,
we praise you.

Exuberant Spirit of God,
speaking words that leap over barriers of mistrust
to convey messages of truth and new understanding,
we praise you.

Exuberant Spirit of God,
flame
          wind
                    speech,
burn, breathe, speak in us;
fill your world with justice and with joy.

Jan Berry, in *Bread of Tomorrow: Prayers for the Church Year*, ed.
Janet Morley (Maryknoll, N.Y.: Orbis; London: Christian Aid,
1992), 129. Used by permission.

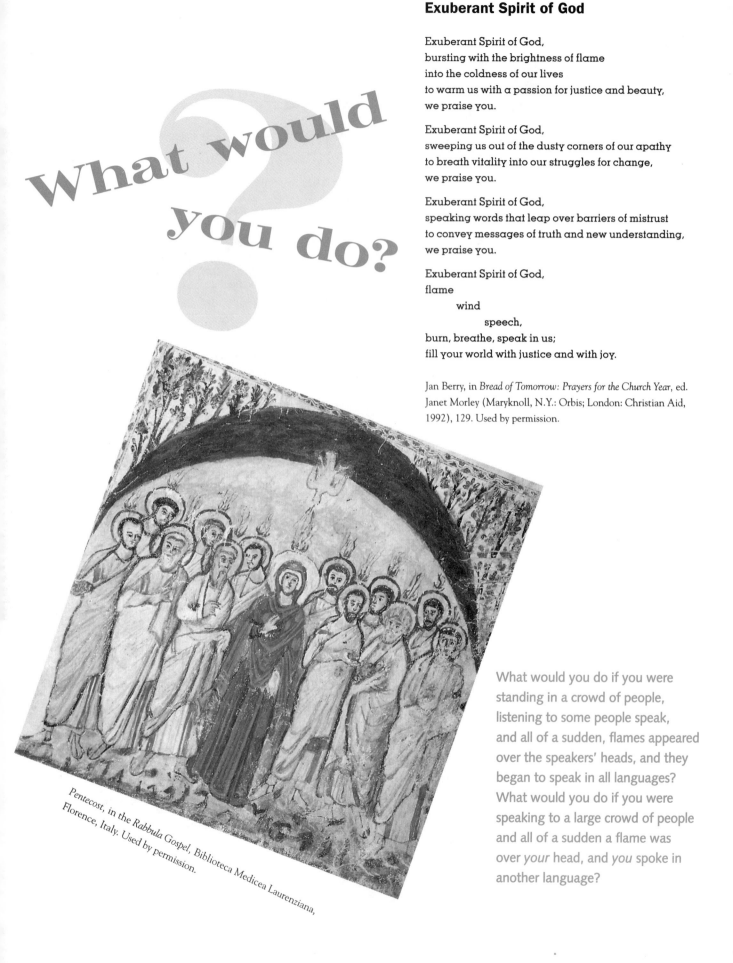

Pentecost, in the *Rabbula Gospel*, Biblioteca Medicea Laurenziana,
Florence, Italy. Used by permission.

What would you do if you were
standing in a crowd of people,
listening to some people speak,
and all of a sudden, flames appeared
over the speakers' heads, and they
began to speak in all languages?
What would you do if you were
speaking to a large crowd of people
and all of a sudden a flame was
over *your* head, and *you* spoke in
another language?

86

And It Was Good

God saw everything that
God had made, and indeed,
it was very good.

Genesis 1:31a

Look at the picture closely.

What in creation and in the
universe is circular or spherical?

How many "gifts" of God's
creation does this picture remind
you of?

Kenneth Noland, *The Gift*, 1961–62, Tate Gallery, London (Art Resource, N.Y.). Used by permission.

All you big things, bless the Lord

Mount Kilimanjaro and Lake Victoria

The Rift Valley and the Serengeti Plain

Fat baobabs and shady mango trees

All eucalyptus and tamarind trees

Bless the Lord

Praise and extol [God] for ever and ever.

All you tiny things, bless the Lord

Busy black ants and hopping fleas

Wriggling tadpoles and mosquito larvae

Flying locusts and water drops

Pollen dust and tsetse flies

Millet seeds and dried dagaa

Bless the Lord

Praise and extol [God] for ever and ever.

"African Canticle," in *Earth Prayers from Around the World,*
ed. Elizabeth Roberts and Elias Amidon (San Francisco:
HarperSanFrancisco, 1991), 219. Used by permission.

Bless the Lord, O my soul

Lord my God you are great

    You are clothed with the energy of atoms

    as with a mantle

From a cloud of whirling cosmic dust

as on the potter's wheel

you began to tease out the whorls of galaxies

and the gas escapes from your fingers condensing and

    burning

as you were fashioning the stars

You made a spatterdash of planets like spores or seeds

and scattered the comets like flowers. . . .

Ernesto Cardenal, in *Earth Prayers from Around the World*,
ed. Elizabeth Roberts and Elias Amidon
(San Francisco: HarperSanFrancisco, 1991), 224.
Used by permission.

you will be a blessing

Now God said to Abram, "Go from your country and your kindred and your parents' house to the land that I will show you. I will make of you a great nation,

and I will bless you, and make your name great, so that you will be a blessing and in you all the families of the earth shall be blessed." So Abram went, as God had told him.

Genesis 12:1–2, 3b–4a

Jacopo Bassano, *Abraham's Journey*, Staatliche Museum, Berlin Germany.

I believe

What does it feel like to leave a familiar place, and familiar people? How does having to move call us to hear and experience God's promise of blessing?

[God,] you have always mapped out tomorrow's road: and, although it is hidden, today I believe.

Jefferey W. Rowthorn, *The Wideness of God's Mercy: Litanies to Enlarge Our Prayer* (Minneapolis: The Seabury Press, 1985), 1:47. Used by permission.

John Mix Stanley, *Oregon City on the Willamette River*, c. 1850–1852, oil on canvas,
Amon Carter Museum, Fort Worth Texas. Used by permission.

give us courage

How can the same land be a blessing for two peoples? How can two peoples be blessings for each other?

Creator of the universe, infinite and glorious,
you give us laws to save us from our folly;
give us eyes to see your plan unfolding,
your purpose emerging as the world is made;
give us courage to follow the truth,
courage to go where you lead;
then we shall know blessings beyond our dreams;
then will your will be done.

New Zealand Book of Prayer: The Church of the Province of New Zealand
(Auckland, New Zealand: William Collins Publishers, Ltd., 1989), 465.
Used by permission.

Laugh with Me

Abraham was a hundred years old when his son Isaac was born to him. Now Sarah said, "God has brought laughter for me; everyone who hears will laugh with me."

Genesis 21:5–6

Rembrandt Harmensz van Rijn, *Abraham Entertaining the Three Angels*, 1656, private collection.

Abraham and Sarah enjoyed an unexpected gift from God. What unexpected gifts have you enjoyed? Why do you think it's important to "expect the unexpected"?

We can laugh with Sarah over the joy of new life in her. We can also laugh with joy because of the promise this new life represents for us. O God, go with us now, and help us watch for your unexpected gifts. Help us laugh with you and with each other when we find your surprises. **Amen.**

Rembrandt Harmensz van Rijn,
Abraham Entertaining the Three Angels, detail, 1656,
private collection.

Sarah
from *Sarah Laughed*

The following is taken from a rhythmically spoken piece for narrator, two speaking choirs, and a congregation (split into four sections).

Part 4

Old Sarah	Weak Sarah
Elderly	Ancient
Geriatric	Grey-haired
Wrinkled	Fading
Wasting	Weakening
Getting on in years	Over the hill

YES!
She shall bear a son.

Narrator:
And Abraham fell on his face…and laughed!

Congregation Section 1: Ha-ha *(continues)*
Congregation Section 2: Hee-hee *(adding to above)*
Congregation Section 3: Ho-ho *(adding to above)*
Congregation Section 4: Yuk-yuk *(adding to above)*

Part 5

Narrator: Time went by.
The Word came again

to Sarah	by three angels
behind a tent	out of sight

Both sides: A child shall be *born!*

Part 6

Narrator: And it began to bubble up…
that laugh again

She giggled	she shook
she tittered	she snickered
she chortled	she cackled
she crowed	she held her sides

She burst out laughing!

Congregation Section 1: Ha-ha *(continues)*
Congregation Section 2: Hee-hee *(adding to above)*
Congregation Section 3: Ho-ho *(adding to above)*
Congregation Section 4: Yuk-yuk *(adding to above)*

Part 7

Limp with laughter	rolling on the floor
rejoicing	delighted
exulting	jubilant
elated	flushed
whoopee	hurrah

Both sides: huzzah-huzzah

yippee	yea rah
hosanna	hallelujah

Both sides: hallel
Is anything too wonderful for God?

Judy Gattis Smith,
Copyright © 1993. All rights reserved.
Used by permission.

laugh!

Baptized into New Life

Therefore we have been buried with Christ by baptism into death, so that, just as Christ was raised from the dead by the glory of God, so we too might walk in newness of life.

Romans 6:4

This baby is about to be baptized, probably by sprinkling or pouring. Is this a familiar scene in your church? What do you think the parents and sponsors are thinking?

Harriet Backer, *Baptism in Tanum Church, 1892*, detail, Nasjonalgalleriet, Oslo, Norway. Photograph © J. Lathion. Used by permission.

Prayer

O Life that surges through all living things and is their Source, we confess that we have often closed ourselves off and prevented the river flow of life through us. We have lost touch with the unique worth of the life each of us has to live. Our eyes fail to perceive beauty in people and in the world. Open our eyes, that we may walk in newness of life through One who is the Resurrection and the Life. Amen.

Ruth C. Duck in Bread for the Journey: Resources for Worship *(New York: The Pilgrim Press, 1981), 58. Used by permission.*

Affirmation of Baptism

Leader: Do you desire to affirm your baptism into the faith and family of Jesus Christ?

Group: I do.

Leader: Do you renounce the powers of evil and desire the freedom of new life in Christ?

Group: I do.

Leader: Do you profess Jesus Christ as . . . Savior?

Group: I do.

*Leader: Do you promise, by the grace of God,
to be Christ's disciple,
to follow in the way of our Savior,
to resist oppression and evil,
to show love and justice,
and to witness to the work and
word of Jesus Christ
as best you are able?*

Group: I promise, with the help of God.

*Leader: Do you promise,
according to the grace given you,
to grow in the Christian faith
and to be a faithful member
of the church of Jesus Christ,
celebrating Christ's presence
and furthering Christ's mission in
all the world?*

Group: I promise, with the help of God.

Book of Worship: United Church of Christ (New York: United Church of Christ Office for Church Life and Leadership, 1986), 161. Used by permission.

Share in Christ's baptism.

This newly baptized person has been immersed in the river. Jesus was baptized in this way. Have you been part of a baptism like this one?

David Alan Harvey, *Baptism*, © National Geographic Society, Washington, D.C. Used by permission.

United Church of Christ Statement of Faith in the Form of a Doxology

We believe in you, O God, Eternal Spirit,
God of our Savior Jesus Christ and our God,
and to your deeds we testify:

    You call the worlds into being,
        create persons in your own image,
        and set before each one the ways of life and death.

    You seek in holy love to save all people from
    aimlessness and sin.

    You judge people and nations by your righteous will
    declared through prophets and apostles.

    In Jesus Christ, the man of Nazareth, our crucified
    and risen Savior,
        you have come to us
        and shared our common lot,
        conquering sin and death
        and reconciling the world to yourself.

    You bestow upon us your Holy Spirit,
        creating and renewing the church of Jesus Christ,
        binding in covenant faithful people of all ages,
        tongues, and races.

    You call us into your church
        to accept the cost and joy of discipleship,
        to be your servants in the service of others,
        to proclaim the gospel to all the world
        and resist the powers of evil,
        to share in Christ's baptism and eat at his table,
        to join him in his passion and victory.

    You promise to all who trust you
        forgiveness of sins and fullness of grace,
        courage in the struggle for justice and peace,
        your presence in trial and rejoicing,
        and eternal life in your realm which has no end.

Blessing and honor, glory and power be unto you.
Amen.

Book of Worship: United Church of Christ (New York: United Church of Christ Office for Church Life and Leadership, 1986), 514. Used by permission.

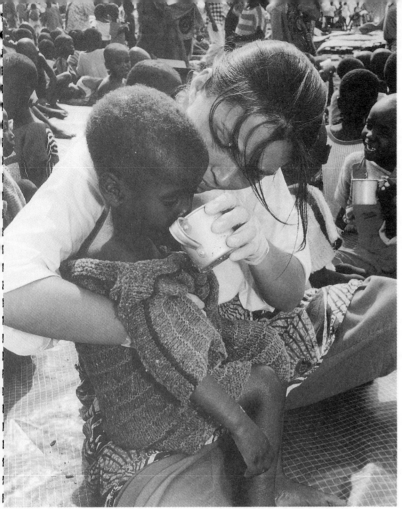

John Hopper, *Rwandan Starving Children*,
© AP/Wide World Photos, N.Y. Used by permission.

Even a Cup of COLD WATER

Jesus said, "Whoever welcomes you welcomes me, and whoever welcomes me welcomes the one who sent me, and whoever gives even a cup of cold water to one of these little ones in the name of a disciple—truly I tell you, none of these will lose their reward."

Matthew 10:40, 42

What is the hungriest and thirstiest you can ever remember being? Most of us have never known starvation, and although we may have said at times "I'm dying of thirst," we weren't really. But can you remember a hot day when someone offered you a cold glass of lemonade or some ice water? On a bitterly cold day do you remember how much you appreciated being offered a cup of hot chocolate? Even small gestures like these are acts of hospitality. Can you think of other ways to extend hospitality to someone who is "thirsty"?

WHEN I WAS A STRANGER

Jesus said: Behold, I stand at the door and knock.
Enter! We greet and welcome you. Can we get you anything?
Please: A family of refugees has just arrived and needs so much.
**We'll collect food and furniture and clothes
for them, and help them learn English.**
Listen: A new kid is facing his first day at your school tomorrow.
**We'll smile and say hi and invite him to join
us for lunch.**
Wait: An elderly widower is feeling sad and lonely.
We'll ask him to our family's picnic!
See: A child is thirsty.
We'll pour her a glass of cold water, and ask if she wants more.
Well done, welcomers: Whatever hospitality you offer to these,
you offer to me.

Love Bade Me Welcome

Love bade me welcome: yet my soul drew back,
  Guilty of dust and sin.
But quick-ey'd Love, observing me grow slack
  From my first entrance in,
Drew nearer to me, sweetly questioning
  If I lack'd anything.

A guest, I answer'd, worthy to be here:
  Love said, you shall be he.
I the unkind, ungrateful? Ah, my dear,
  I cannot look on thee.
Love took my hand, and smiling did reply,
  Who made the eyes but I?

Truth Lord, but I have marr'd them: let my shame
  Go where it doth deserve.
And know you not, says Love, who bore the blame?
  My dear, then I will serve.
You must sit down, says Love, and taste my meat.
  So I did sit and eat.

George Herbert, from *Five Mystical Songs*, distributed in
the U.S. by Galaxy Music Corp.

**In this poem, which was set to music,
"I" (the narrator) receives a taste of divine
hospitality. Re-read the words, substituting
the word "Jesus" for "Love" and "my Savior" or
"dear Christ" for "my dear." Does the meaning
become clearer? In the seventeenth century
when George Herbert wrote this, it was not
uncommon to slightly veil religious words
with symbolic synonyms rather than write
"God" or "Jesus" outright. Do you prefer
the more subtle or the more direct
way of poetic expression?**

A Hospitality Checklist

Check off the people to whom you would like to extend hospitality.

Put a star next to one to whom you actually will offer hospitality this week,

or as soon as possible.

_____ someone who can't get out of the house

_____ a "latchkey" child in the neighborhood

_____ an older person who lives alone

_____ a visitor at church or youth group

_____ a new kid at camp or school

_____ an international student

_____ someone who looks lost and needs directions

_____ a new family

_____ someone with a disability

_____ a person of a different racial or ethnic background from mine

_____ other _____ (you decide)

Check off the gestures of hospitality you are willing to offer.

_____ going shopping for groceries and other necessities

_____ childcare or pet care

_____ transportation

_____ a meal with your family

_____ playing games or sports with them

_____ speaking to them, showing interest in them

_____ going to the library with or for them

_____ cooking or baking for or with them

_____ reading to them

_____ introducing them to friends, inviting them along

_____ other _____

WELCOME

I Will Give You

Rest

Come to me, all you that are weary and are carrying heavy burdens, and I will give you rest. Take my yoke upon you, and learn from me; for I am gentle and humble in heart, and you will find rest for your souls. For my yoke is easy, and my burden is light.

Matthew 11:28–30

Henry Moore, *Memorial Figure*, 1945-6, *Horton Stone*, as reproduced in Henry Moore and John Hedgecoe, *Henry Moore: My Ideas, Inspiration and Life as an Artist* (London: Ebury Press), 195. Used by permission.

Things That Make Me Weary

In this space, list things (or even people) that seem like heavy burdens and tire you out.

In the space below, write a prayer asking Jesus to give you rest from one or more of the wearisome things you listed.

Does this figure look "at rest" to you?
What do you think of when you hear the word "rest"?
Compare it to the cartoon on the next page.
Which image of "rest" seems more like what Jesus meant?

Calvin and Hobbes, from *Scientific Progress Goes "Boink,"* copyright © 1991 by Bill Watterson.
Reprinted by permission of Universal Press Syndicate. All rights reserved.

Have you ever looked at a sleeping cat? When was the last time you felt as "pooped" as Hobbes appears to be? Are you able to rest from your labors and burdens, or do they build up so you feel exhausted all the time?

Give Us Rest

Group 1: When we are carrying heavy loads,

Group 2: O God, give us rest.

Group 3: When we are exhausted from a hard day's work,

Group 1: O God who never wearies, give us rest.

Group 2: When we feel the stress of too much to think about,

Group 3: O God who never wearies, give us rest.

Group 1: When we grieve for ourselves or for others,

Group 2: O God who never wearies, give us rest.

Group 3: When we think we can't go on,

Group 1: O God who never wearies, give us rest.

Group 2: When we feel alone,

Group 3: O God who never wearies, give us rest.

Group 1: When we feel far away from you,

Group 2: O God who never wearies, give us rest.

Group 3: When we feel guilty about a wrong we have done,

Group 1: O God who never wearies, give us rest.

Group 2: When we are treated unjustly,

Group 3: O God who never wearies, give us rest.

Group 1: When we ask for your help,

Group 2: O God who never wearies, give us rest.

A Sower Went Out to Sow

And Jesus told them many things in parables, saying: "Listen! A sower went out to sow."

Matthew 13:3

Vincent van Gogh, *The Sower*, Rijksmuseum Kroeller-Mueller, Otterlo, The Netherlands (Erich Lessing/Art Resource, N.Y.). Used by permission.

Let Me Tell You a Story

Refrain:
Let me tell you a story, come and follow me:
    out of the tomb, down from the tree.
Peter, Joanna, Martha, Zacchaeus,
    come, come, come and follow me.

A man went up to Jericho . . .
    There was a father who had two sons . . .
A sower went out to sow . . .
    In those days a decree went out . . .

Repeat Refrain

Fell into the hands of robbers . . .
    He would gladly eat what the pigs eat . . .

Some fell on stony ground . . .
    There were shepherds keeping watch . . .

Repeat Refrain

Which one was the neighbor?
    My child who was lost is found.
Some fell on good soil.
    We have seen the star in the east!

Repeat Refrain

Vincent van Gogh, *Wheat Field with Crows*, Van Gogh Museum, Amsterdam, The Netherlands (Art Resource, N.Y.). Used by permission.

Reflect on the parable of the sower. What parts of the parable can you identify in both paintings by the same artist?

Tell me, tell me

Vincent van Gogh (1853-1890) was born and raised in Holland, the son and grandson of ministers. In his youth Vincent tried to make a living as a teacher, an art gallery salesman, and a missionary. All of these careers turned out to be dead ends. His frustrated father considered Vincent "rocky soil," in which nothing seemed to take root.

the stories . . .

At age 27, after bitterly renouncing his past life, including the church, Vincent resolved to become an artist. Until the end of his life, ten years later, he was consumed by the passion to paint. Disdaining "polite" society, he preferred to live among the peasants and paint common people, fields, and flowers. He often used the theme of sowing and harvesting in his paintings. He once said to a friend, "Gusts of remembrance from former days and my aspirations to the infinite symbolized by the sower and the sheaf still fascinate me as much as ever."

Wheat or Weeds?

Let both the wheat and weeds grow together until the harvest; and at harvest time I will tell the reapers, Collect the weeds first and bind them in bundles to be burned, but gather the wheat into my barn.

Matthew 13:30

Have you ever done any farm work or gardening? If you have, you know about weeds! What would happen if no one was there to harvest the crops and remove the weeds? Why does the householder tell the workers not to gather the weeds? What does this mean for the wheat?

Patrick DesJarlait, *Gathering Wild Rice*, The Heard Museum, Phoenix, Arizona. Used by permission of the Patrick DesJarlait Estate.

Can you understand why Huck would rather go to "the bad place," where Miss Watson says his buddy, the "bad boy" Tom Sawyer, will likely end up? What do you think of Miss Watson's description of heaven?

Then [Miss Watson] told me all about the bad place, and I said I wished I was there. She got mad, then, but I didn't mean no harm. All I wanted was to go somewheres; all I wanted was a change, I warn't particular. She said it was wicked to say what I said; said she wouldn't say it for the whole world; *she* was going to live so as to go to the good place. Well, I couldn't see no advantage in going where she was going, so I made up my mind I wouldn't try for it. But I never said so, because it would only make trouble, and wouldn't do no good.

Now she had got a start, and she went on and told me all about the good place. She said all a body would have to do there was to go around all day long with a harp and sing, forever and ever. So I didn't think much of it. But I never said so. I asked her if she reckoned Tom Sawyer would go there, and she said not by a considerable sight. I was glad about that, because I wanted him and me to be together.

Mark Twain [Samuel Langhorne Clemens], *The Adventures of Huckleberry Finn* (New York: Penguin Books, 1985).

The Garden of Live Flowers

"Oh, Tiger Lily," said Alice, addressing herself to one that was waving gracefully about in the wind, "I *wish* you could talk!"

"We *can* talk," said the Tiger Lily, "when there is anybody worth talking to."

Alice was so astonished that she couldn't speak for a minute; it quite seemed to take her breath away.

At length, as the Tiger Lily only went on waving about, she spoke again, in a timid voice—almost in a whisper. "And can *all* the flowers talk?"

"As well as *you* can," said the Tiger Lily, "and a great deal louder."

"It isn't manners for us to begin, you know," said the Rose, "and I really was wondering when you'd speak! Said I to myself, 'Her face has got *some* sense in it, though it's not a clever one!' Still, you're the right color, and that goes a long way."

"I don't care about the color," the Tiger Lily remarked. "If only her petals curled up a little more, she'd be all right." . . .

"I never saw anybody that looked stupider," a Violet said, so suddenly that Alice quite jumped; for it hadn't spoken before.

"Hold *your* tongue!" cried the Tiger Lily. "As if *you* ever saw anybody!

> At some time in your life you may have felt like Alice, being judged by others who "don't have a clue" what you're all about. Should she feel like a weed, just because the flowers don't know how else to classify her? Have you ever been like these flowers, judging someone's value based on very little knowledge?

You keep your head under the leaves, and snore away there, till you know no more what's going on in the world than if you were a bud!"

"Are there any more people in the garden besides me?" Alice said. . . .

"There's one other flower in the garden that can move about like you," said the Rose.

"I wonder how you do it—" ("You're always wondering," said the Tiger Lily.) "But she's more bushy than you are."

"Is she like me?" Alice asked eagerly, for the thought crossed her mind, "There's another little girl in the garden somewhere!"

"Well, she has the same awkward shape as you," the Rose said, "but she's redder—and her petals are shorter, I think—"

"Her petals are done up close, almost like a dahlia," the Tiger Lily interrupted; "not tumbled about anyhow, like yours."

"But that's not *your* fault," the Rose added kindly; "you're beginning to fade, you know—and then one can't help one's petals getting a little untidy!"

Lewis Carroll, *Alice in Wonderland* (New York: Atheneum, 1994).

Parables of

God's Dominion

"The dominion of heaven is like . . ."

Matthew 13:33a

. . . yeast that a woman took and mixed in with three measures of flour until all of it was leavened.

God longs for God
and uses us,
rises in us . . .
becomes in us.

Let us be silent,
a quiet dough

where God moves
into every pore . . .
where God lives
as God pleases.

Let us rise simply.
a quiet dough.

Gunilla Norris, "The Second Rising,"
in *Becoming Bread: Meditations on Loving and Transformation* (New York: Crown Publishers, 1993), 56. Used by permission.

Jan Vermeer, *Woman Holding a Balance*, Widener Collection, National Gallery of Art, Smithsonian Institution, Washington, D.C. © 1994 Board of Trustees, National Gallery of Art, Smithsonian Institution. Used by permission.

One Pearl of Great Value

A condition of complete simplicity

(Costing not less than everything)

And all shall be well and

all manner of things shall be well.

T. S. Eliot, excerpt from "Little Gidding," in *Four Quartets* (New York: Harcourt Brace Jovanovich, 1943), 39. Copyright 1943 by T. S. Eliot and renewed 1971 by Esme Valerie Eliot. Used by permission of Harcourt Brace & Co.

. . . a merchant in search of fine pearls.

Ozymandias

I met a traveller from an antique land

Who said: Two vast and trunkless legs of stone

Stand in the desert. . . . Near them, on the sand,

Half sunk, a shattered visage lies, whose frown,

And wrinkled lip, and sneer of cold command,

Tell that its sculptor well those passions read

Which yet survive, stamped on these lifeless things,

The hand that mocked them, and the heart that fed:

And on the pedestal these words appear:

"My name is Ozymandias, king of kings:

Look on my works, ye Mighty, and despair!"

Nothing beside remains. Round the decay

Of that colossal wreck, boundless and bare

The lone and level sands stretch far away.

Percy Bysshe Shelley (1792–1822)

What is the dominion of God *like?*

Ozymandias is the Greek name for Ramses II, the Egyptian ruler in the thirteenth century B.C.E., who is said to have had a huge statue carved of himself. Of that statue, the traveller relates that only the broken-off head and legs survived. The "works" of the pharaoh have disappeared with "the sands of time." What do you think of the writing on the pedestal? What does the poem suggest about earthly dominions?

FACE to FACE encounter

Jacob was left alone; and a man wrestled with him until daybreak. So Jacob called the place Peniel, saying, "For I have seen God face to face and yet my life is preserved."

Genesis 32:24, 30

Paul Gauguin, *Vision After the Sermon (Jacob Wrestling the Angel),* detail, 1888, National Gallery of Scotland, Edinburgh, Great Britain (Bridgeman/Art Resource, N.Y.). Used by permission.

Wrestling

In your own life experience, what might be an example of "wrestling with an angel"? How do you know whether your opponent has your best interests in mind? Consider the person who struggles with an addiction. Compare that with the struggle to overcome poverty or injustice or to make a difficult moral decision.

Come, O Thou Traveler Unknown

Come, O thou Traveler unknown,
  whom still I hold, but cannot see!
My company before is gone,
  And I am left alone with thee.
With thee all night I mean to stay,
  and wrestle till the break of day;
With thee all night I mean to stay,
  and wrestle till the break of day.

I need not tell thee who I am,
  my misery and sin declare;
thyself hast called me by my name,
  look on thy hands and read it there.
But who, I ask thee, who art thou?
  Tell me thy name, and tell me now.
But who, I ask thee, who art thou?
  Tell me thy name, and tell me now.

Yield to me now, for I am weak,
  but confident in self-despair!
Speak to my heart, in blessing speak,
  be conquered by my instant prayer.
Speak, or thou never hence shall move,
  and tell me if thy name is Love.
Speak, or thou never hence shall move,
  and tell me if thy name is Love.

'Tis Love! 'tis Love! Thou diedst for me,
  I hear thy whisper in my heart.
The morning breaks, the shadows flee,
  pure, Universal Love thou art.
To me, to all, thy mercies move;
  thy nature and thy name is Love.
To me, to all, thy mercies move;
  thy nature and thy name is Love.

Charles Wesley, 1742

Penny Tweedie. © Tony Stone Images. Used by permission.

What do you think is going through this person's mind?

Psalm 17 Litany

Group 1: Hear a just cause, O God; attend to my cry; give ear to my prayer from lips free of deceit. From you let my vindication come; let your eyes see the right.

Group 2: As for me, I shall behold your face in righteousness; when I awake I shall be satisfied, beholding your likeness.

Group 3: If you try my heart, if you visit me by night, if you test me, you will find no wickedness in me; my mouth does not transgress. As for what others do, by the word of your lips I have avoided the ways of the violent. My steps have held fast to your paths; my feet have not slipped.

Group 1: As for me, I shall behold your face in righteousness; when I awake I shall be satisfied, beholding your likeness.

Group 2: I call upon you, for you will answer me, O God; incline your ear to me, hear my words. Wondrously show your steadfast love, O Savior of those who seek refuge from their adversaries at your right hand.

Group 3: As for me, I shall behold your face in righteousness; when I awake I shall be satisfied, beholding your likeness.

You of Little Faith

Jesus said, "Come." So Peter got out of the boat, started walking on the water, and came toward Jesus. But when he noticed the strong wind, he became frightened.

Matthew 14:29–30a

Henry O. Tanner, *Christ Walking on Water*, 1910, Evans-Tibbs Collection of Afro-American Art, Washington, D.C. Used by permission.

Imagine

that you are in this painting.

Where are you?

What are you feeling and thinking?

How much faith

would it take to get out of the boat in the storm?

John Pitman Weber, *Yell*, 1990, Oak Park, Illinois. Used by permission.

Why do you suppose the person is yelling? What does the picture make you think of?
Think about the disciple Peter looking at this painting and thinking about his experience
on the lake. What would you think about if you were Peter?

Litany of Peter

Lord, save me !

Reader 1: Peter left the boat and walked on the water toward Jesus.

Reader 2: But the wind distracted him; he took his eyes off Jesus.

Reader 3: Peter was scared and started to sink.

Reader 1: Lord, save me!

Reader 2: We can walk on water toward Jesus.

Reader 3: But sometimes day-to-day things distract us and we take our eyes off Jesus.

Reader 1: We get scared and start to sink.

Reader 2: Lord, save us!

Reader 3: We forget to keep Jesus in front of us.

Reader 1: We forget to hold on.

Reader 2: We let our fear get the best of us.

Reader 3: Lord, save us!

Reader 1: I believe that Jesus will be with me in the storm.

Reader 2: I believe that Jesus will keep me from sinking.

Reader 3: I believe that Jesus can help me walk on water.

All: Thank you, Lord!

How very good and pleasant it is when kindred live together in unity!

Psalm 133:1

Palmer Hayden, *Midsummer Night in Harlem*, The African-American Museum, Los Angeles. Used by permission.

Life Together

I must give the people around me credit for encouraging me for doing the right thing in the right way. I don't know what would have happened if they had said, "That's not the way to do it." . . . In retrospect [Harlem] was a great community; it was a very fascinating community. If you had asked me this forty years ago, I wouldn't have used these terms. . . . It was a very cohesive community. You knew people. You didn't know their names, but you'd pass people on the street and see the face over and over again. . . . You knew the police, you knew the firemen, you knew the teachers, the people on the street. You knew the peddlar. It was *me*.

Jacob Lawrence, *Toussaint L'Ouverture Series Catalogue*, ed. James Buell
(New York: United Church Board for Homeland Ministries, 1982), 21.

Through his use of space and his manner of grouping figures together, the artist conveys the impression that everyone in this painting is "family." Have you ever been part of a scene like this one? Who are your "kindred"?

Hine Ma Tov
(How Good and Pleasant it is)

Words: Psalm 133:1   Music: Israeli round

Part 1 *Quickly, with energy*

Unison

Hi - ne ma tov u - ma na - im
How ver - y good and how plea - sant

she - vet a - chim gam ya chad.
when kin - dred sit to - geth - er;

Part 2

Hi - ne ma tov
To dwell as one,

u - ma na - im.
how ver - y good it is.

Palmer Hayden, *Midsummer Night in Harlem*, detail, The African-American Museum, Los Angeles. Used by permission.

To sing this as a round, divide into two groups. Groups A sings Part 1 twice, then Part 2 twice. Groups B sings Part 1 as Group A sings Part 2.

UNITY

God of all, source and goal of community, whose will is that all your people enjoy fullness of life, may we be builders of community, caring for your good earth here and worldwide, that we may delight in diversity and choose solidarity, for you are in community with us, our God, forever. Amen.

Anonymous

110

We, who are many, are one body in Christ, and individually we are members one of another.

Romans 12:5

"The word became flesh." That is the center of the Christian message. Often the body was seen as a hindrance to the full realization of what the word wanted to express. But Jesus confronts us with the word that can be seen, heard, and touched. The body thus becomes the way to know the word and to enter into relationship with the word. The body of Jesus becomes the way of life.

Henri Nouwen, *The Road to Daybreak: A Spiritual Journey* (New York: Doubleday, 1988), 150–51. Used by permission of Bantam Doubleday Dell Publishing Group, Inc.

We, Who Are Many —One Body

Hildegard of Bingen, *All Creatures Celebrate*, illumination 15, as reproduced in Matthew Fox, *Illuminations of Hildegard of Bingen* (Santa Fe: Bear & Co., 1985). Used by permission.

Because I am a Christian and because I think my own family of faith needs to learn inclusiveness perhaps more than any other. . . . It is my conviction that . . . a conscious cooperation infused with the Holy Spirit calls us toward . . . a relationship to God and the world that does not try to make things easy by ruling out whole areas of human experience and whole groups of human beings. . . . Church members may rejoice that we are being offered the opportunity to move toward wholeness—not just the wholeness of Christ's body, the church, but also our own internal wholeness.

Virginia Mollenkott, *Godding: Human Responsibility and the Bible* (New York: Crossroad, 1987), 39.

What Are
My Gifts?

Look at all
the different
kinds of talents.

Mark anything you're good at.
Are there other things you are
interested in learning?
Make a note of talents you have
that aren't represented here.

_____

_____

_____

_____

Prayer

We thank you, O God Within and
Beyond us,
for linking our lives
in so many ways,
making a chain of hope
and compassion
long enough
and strong enough
to circle the globe.
When we walk hand in hand,
when we work side by side,
the impossible becomes
the next challenge before us,
and we know we can do
what we dared not attempt.
May mountains of misery melt
with Your Word of concern
which we put into action,
and may there never again
be despair or denial
of Your saving grace.
Amen.

Miriam Therese Winter, *WomanWord:
A Feminist Lectionary and Psalter*
(New York: Crossroad, 1990), 237.
© Medical Mission Sisters, 1990.
Used by permission.

takes talent

there are two
kinds of human
beings in the world
so my observation
has told me
namely and to wit
as follows
firstly
those who
even though they
were to reveal
the secret of the universe
to you would fail
to impress you
with any sense
of the importance
of the news
and secondly
those who could
communicate to you
that they had
just purchased
ten cents worth
of paper napkins
and make you
thrill and vibrate
with the intelligence

      archy

Don Marquis, *The Lives and Times
of Archy and Mehitabel* (New York:
Doubleday and Company, 1927).
Copyright © 1927, 1930, 1933,
1935, 1950 by Doubleday, a division
of Bantam Doubleday Dell Publishing
Group, Inc. Used by permission of
Doubleday, a division of Bantam
Doubleday Dell Publishing Group, Inc.